Punch Lines

A collection of one-liners,
sentence-sermons, and attention-getters.

Curtis Hutson

SWORD of the LORD
PUBLISHERS
P. O. BOX 1099, MURFREESBORO, TN 37133

Printed and Bound in the United States of America

Introduction

Great truths well stated are easy to remember and make great teaching tools. Many of the major doctrines I have learned came from simple, short statements well put. We have collected and use such statements with great effect in our own ministry. One man said, "I would come to hear you preach just to get the nuggets that you put out in the course of a sermon."

This book contains many nuggets which we have gleaned from reading and listening, nuggets that the pastor, Sunday school teacher, conference speaker, or evangelist will find useful in spicing up a sermon and helping to hold the attention of a congregation.

We have given credit when the source of the statement was known. Many of the statements are by Dr. Bob Jones, Sr., who was well-known for his "Chapel Sayings" and, in our opinion, is the most quotable preacher we have ever heard speak or have ever read. We have often used his "Chapel Sayings" with great profit and blessing to our own hearers. Some of the statements in the book were taken from our sermons which were published in THE SWORD OF THE LORD or Sword books. A few of these one-liners, sentence sermons, or attention-getters are humorous, though it is not the intention of the author to compile a book on humor. We plan to do that later.

We trust the dear Lord will use this compilation to make every sincere preacher and Bible teacher more effective in communicating the great truths of the Bible.

Curtis W. Hutson, Editor
Sword of the Lord

Table of Contents

Bible

Some Christians are so ignorant about the Bible, they think an epistle is an apostle's wife.

THE BIBLE BELT NEEDS ANOTHER BELT WITH THE BIBLE.

Thumb prints in the Bible are more beneficial than footprints on the moon.

One evidence of the value of the Bible is the character of those who oppose it.

The Bible is not a science book, but it is scientifically correct. And when science contradicts the Bible, it is sooner or later found out not to be true science. —C.W.H.

GOD'S WILL NEVER CONTRADICTS HIS WORD. —C.W.H.

A clean Bible means a lean soul. —D. L. Moody.

When we read the Bible, God talks with us; when we pray, we talk with God; and we need to do most of the listening. —D. L. Moody.

John Watson, enlarging on the thought that the Bible is so simple that a wayfaring man or a fool need not err therein, said, "It is shallow enough so that the most timid swimmer may enjoy its waters without fear, and yet deep enough for the most expert swimmer to enjoy it without touching bottom."

⌐▭┐

THE BIBLE IS, TO MANY, GOD'S UNOPENED LETTER. —Spurgeon.

⌐▭┐

The promises of the Bible are very large; you can lie down and stretch out on them and you can't kick the footboard, scratch the headboard, or touch the railing on either side. —Bud Robinson.

⌐▭┐

He who has the Holy Spirit in his heart and the Scripture in his hands has all he needs. —Alexander Maclaren.

⌐▭┐

It is impossible to mentally or socially enslave a Bible-reading people. —Horace Greely.

⌐▭┐

MEN DO NOT REJECT THE BIBLE BECAUSE IT CONTRADICTS ITSELF BUT BECAUSE IT CONTRADICTS THEM. —*The Defender.*

⌐▭┐

Joshua was a busy man—decisions to make, burdens to bear, and the opposition to meet—but he was still expected to have morning and evening Bible study (see Joshua 1:8).

⌐▭┐

THE BIBLE CAN BE READ THROUGH IN 60 HOURS. —G. Campbell Morgan.

⌐▭┐

If the translators go much farther in revising and modernizing the Scriptures they'll be having the 5,000 fed on a bucket of Kentucky Fried Chicken. —Red O'Donnell.

⌐ɯɯ⌐

Other books were given for our information; the Bible was given for our transformation.

Calvary, the Cross, the Blood

All the suffering that Jesus did at Calvary, He would have done for just one soul. —C.W.H.

⌐ɯɯ⌐

THE CROSS IS THE LAST ARGUMENT OF GOD. —Spurgeon.

⌐ɯɯ⌐

So entirely redeemed are we that not a hair of our head is omitted from the inventory of the possession which He has purchased in purchasing us.

⌐ɯɯ⌐

It took more than nails to hold Jesus to the cross. The bonds of love held Him there. —Rolla O. Swisher.

⌐ɯɯ⌐

If sin is to be paid for, then the finite must suffer infinitely or the Infinite must suffer finitely. —C.W.H.

⌐ɯɯ⌐

Character

Sow a thought, you reap a desire; sow a desire, you reap an act; sow an act, you reap a character; but it all began with a thought.

FOLLOWING THE LINES OF LEAST RESISTANCE MAKES RIVERS AND MEN CROOKED.

Your character is what God knows you to be; your reputation is what men think you are. —Bob Jones, Sr.

No amount of riches can atone for poverty of character.

Back of every tragedy in human character there is a process of wicked thinking. —Bob Jones, Sr.

The happiness of your life depends upon the character of your thoughts. —Marcus Aurelius.

MUCH MAY BE KNOWN OF A MAN'S CHARACTER BY WHAT EXCITES HIS LAUGHTER. —Goethe.

The test of your character is what it takes to stop you. —Bob Jones, Sr.

CHARACTER

Character is simply a habit long continued. —Plutarch.

There are two reasons why a person cannot get credit: Because he is not known, or because he is known.

WHATEVER YOU DISLIKE IN ANOTHER PERSON, BE SURE TO CORRECT IN YOURSELF.

The thing you would do if you could do, in the sight of God you have done. —Bob Jones, Sr.

You are not what you think you are, but you are what you think. "As he thinketh in his heart, so is he" (Prov. 23:7). —C.W.H.

You can borrow brains, but you cannot borrow character. —Bob Jones, Sr.

CHARACTER IS NOT MADE IN A CRISIS—IT IS ONLY EXHIBITED.

Even if I knew that tomorrow the world would go to pieces, I would still plant my little apple tree and pay my debts. — Martin Luther.

Brains and beauty are nature's gifts; character is your own achievement.

WHAT YOU LOVE AND WHAT YOU HATE REVEAL WHAT YOU ARE. —Bob Jones, Sr.

We often dislike people not for what they are but for what we are.

A reputation once broken may possibly be repaired, but the world will always keep its eyes on the spot where the crack was.

Lincoln was great, not because he lived in a log cabin, but because he was able to get out of it.

If honor be your clothing, your suit will last a lifetime; but if clothing be your honor, it will be worn threadbare.

DON'T BLAME THE RULE IF YOU DON'T MEASURE UP.

It isn't what you have, but what you are, that makes life worth living.

A photographer couldn't make a living if he made pictures of people as they really are. —Billy Sunday.

REPUTATION IS PRECIOUS, BUT CHARACTER IS PRICELESS.

It is right to be contented with what you have but never with what you are.

⌐mm⌐

Your strength is seen in what you stand for; your weakness in what you fall for.

⌐mm⌐

Blessed is he who has learned to admire, but not envy; to follow, but not imitate; to praise, but not flatter; to lead, but not manipulate.

Choosing

God loved freedom so much that He allowed Adam and Eve the freedom to make the wrong choice, even when He knew that choice would plunge the whole world into sin. —C.W.H.

⌐mm⌐

God has given us the privilege of making the choices of life, but He sets the consequences. —R. J. Little.

⌐mm⌐

You need not choose evil; you have only to fail to choose good, and you drift fast enough toward evil. —W. J. Dawson.

⌐mm⌐

OUR PRESENT CHOICES DETERMINE OUR PERMANENT CHARACTER!

⌐mm⌐

Learn to say "no." It will be of more use to you than to be able to read Latin. —Spurgeon.

When you have to make a choice and don't make it, that is in itself a choice. —Wm. James.

GOD NEVER BURGLARIZES THE HUMAN WILL. —C.W.H.

Nature gives man corn, but he must grind it; God gives man a will, but he must make the right choices.

Christ, God

Being a Christian is betting your life that there is a God. — George Truett.

IF THE LORD FAILS ME AT THIS TIME, IT WILL BE THE FIRST TIME. —George Mueller.

A girl newly converted gave this as her first testimony: "Jesus is the most unforgettable Person I ever met."

God never sacrifices His justice on the altar of His love. —C.W.H.

God writes with a pen that never blots, speaks with a tongue that never slips, and acts with a hand that never fails.

━━

Everything is needful that He sends; nothing is needful that He withholds. —John Newton.

━━

Grace is God giving Himself for us, and Lordship is our giving ourselves to Him.

━━

GOD MAKES NO MISTAKES! IF YOU THINK HE DOES, THEN YOU ARE MISTAKEN!

━━

When God measures a man, He puts the tape around the heart instead of the head.

━━

The seeking Saviour will never miss a meeting with a seeking sinner. —David R. Anderson.

━━

God is more interested in our holiness than He is our happiness.

━━

IF GOD IS YOUR PARTNER, MAKE YOUR PLANS BIG.

━━

I believe in the virgin birth, the vicarious sufferings, the victorious resurrection and the visible return of Jesus Christ —C.W.H.

━━

Did it ever occur to you that nothing ever occurred to God?

⌐𝗆𝗆⌐

God is more interested in making us what He wants us to be than giving us what we ought to have. —Walter L. Wilson.

Christian Living

Golf is a lot like Christianity—a lot depends on the follow-through.

⌐𝗆𝗆⌐

God always puts omnipotence back of His commands, and we can do anything we ought to do. —Bob Jones, Sr.

⌐𝗆𝗆⌐

THE MAN WHO WALKS WITH GOD ALWAYS KNOWS IN WHAT DIRECTION HE IS GOING.

⌐𝗆𝗆⌐

You can preach a better sermon with your life than with your lips.

⌐𝗆𝗆⌐

Live every day as if it were your last. Do every job as if you were the boss. Drive as if all other vehicles were police cars. Treat everybody else as if he were you.

⌐𝗆𝗆⌐

GOD CALLED US TO PLAY THE GAME, NOT TO KEEP THE SCORE.

⎯⎯

The ambition of every believer should be to seek with every fiber of his being to be like his Lord. —C.W.H.

⎯⎯

Go as far as you can on the right road. —Bob Jones, Sr.

⎯⎯

THE STOPS OF A GOOD MAN, AS WELL AS THE STEPS, ARE ORDERED BY THE LORD.

⎯⎯

The work is solemn—therefore do not trifle. The task is difficult—therefore do not relax. The opportunity is brief—therefore do not delay. The path is narrow—therefore do not wander. The prize is glorious—therefore do not faint. —D. M. Panton.

⎯⎯

No dish ever comes to the table which is so nauseous as cold religion. Put it away! Neither God nor man can endure it. —Spurgeon.

⎯⎯

BE AN "AMEN" CHRISTIAN, BUT DON'T SHOUT IT ANY LOUDER THAN YOU LIVE IT.

⎯⎯

A religion that makes a man look sick certainly won't cure the world. —Phillips Brooks.

⎯⎯

The Scripture gives four names to Christians. . . saints, for their holiness; believers, for their faith; brethren, for their love; disciples, for their knowledge.

⌐᪣⌐

It's best if we are experts at finding the beam in our own eye rather than finding the mote in our brother's eye. —C.W.H.

⌐᪣⌐

THE REWARDS ARE ALWAYS AT THE END OF THE ROAD. IT PAYS TO GO ALL THE WAY WITH JESUS.

⌐᪣⌐

You don't have to have a face so long that you could use it for a fire escape in order to be a Christian.

⌐᪣⌐

Some Christians would make good martyrs: they are so dry they would burn well. —Spurgeon.

⌐᪣⌐

NO MAN EVER GOT LOST ON A STRAIGHT ROAD. —Abraham Lincoln.

⌐᪣⌐

Christianity is a religion of paradoxes. The way up is down; the way to get is to give; the way to be first is to be last; and the way to live is to die. —C.W.H.

⌐᪣⌐

The deeper we go with God in personal experience, the deeper will be our consciousness of sin as well as of God's mercy.

⌐᪣⌐

A Christian will not amount to much unless there is enthusiasm in his Christianity.

DELAYED OBEDIENCE IS DISOBEDIENCE.

Some Christians look like they have been weened on dill pickle juice and had wild persimmons for breakfast. —C.W.H.

The Bible says that Christians are "living stones." But some long-faced church members remind one more of "tombstones."

What makes the Dead Sea dead? Because it is all the time receiving, but never giving out. Why is it that many Christians are cold? Because they are all the time receiving, but never giving out. —D. L. Moody.

WE MUST REALIZE OUR HELPLESSNESS BEFORE GOD CAN USE US.

A Christian is not perfect; he is FORGIVEN.

When there is a good, straight road to the right place, why go a roundabout way to get to that place? —Bob Jones, Sr.

For a Christian, life is not divided into the secular and the sacred. To him all ground is holy ground, every bush a burning bush, every place a temple of worship. —Bob Jones, Sr.

⌐₥┐

CHRISTIANITY HELPS US TO FACE THE MUSIC EVEN WHEN WE DON'T LIKE THE TUNE.

⌐₥┐

There are two *C's* that characterize the Christian life: either *c*hange or *c*hastisement.

⌐₥┐

You don't have to look like you just fell out of the back end of a hearse to be a Christian.

⌐₥┐

You may never do everything you dream you'll do, but you'll never do any more than you dream. So dream and dream big. It costs no more to shoot at eagles than it does at skunks. —C.W.H.

⌐₥┐

The best way to know God's will is to say "I will" to God.

⌐₥┐

PERIODICAL GODLINESS IS PERPETUAL HYPOCRISY.—Spurgeon.

⌐₥┐

It is Christlike to see something in the other fellow that is better than the things you see in yourself. —Uncle Bud Robinson.

⌐₥┐

It is a great deal better to live a holy life than to talk about it. Lighthouses don't ring bells and fire cannons to call attention to their shining; they just shine. —D. L. Moody.

⌐₥┐

A LONG FACE IS A POOR SIGNBOARD FOR JESUS. —John R. Rice.

Civilized man has learned how to fly, but he has lost the art of walking with God!

Some Christians are not only like salt that has lost its savor, but like pepper that has lost its pep.

To grow in grace, pray for people you don't like. If tempted to be afraid in the dark, try better living when the sun is shining. Cold hearts never receive warm blessings.

Young people, there is not a dirty spot on the page of tomorrow. —Bob Jones, Sr.

No man in this life has ever reached the place beyond which there is no opportunity for improvement. —C.W.H.

TOO MANY CHRISTIANS ARE LIKE ARCTIC RIVERS—FROZEN AT THE MOUTH.

We should not ask, "How far can I go into the world and still be a Christian?" but rather, "How near can I live to God?"

So I'll go on not knowing;
I would not if I might;
I'd rather walk with Christ in the dark
Than to walk alone in the light.

Too many of us hear without heeding, read without responding, confess without changing, profess without practicing, worship without witnessing, and seek without sharing. — Wm. Arthur Ward.

⸺

Without God we should fear to move; but when He bids us go, it is dangerous to tarry.

⸺

A CHRISTIAN SHOWS WHAT HE IS BY WHAT HE DOES WITH WHAT HE HAS.

⸺

So live that when people speak evil of you, no one will believe it.

⸺

It is easier to do that which God gives us to do, no matter how hard it is, than to face the reponsibilities of not doing it. — J. R. Miller.

The Church

There are three groups of people in a church: the plus-plus crowd: "I can do it, and you can do it, and let's get it done"; the plus-minus crowd: "I can do it, and you can't do it, so get out of my way and I will do it"; the minus-minus crowd: "I can't do it, and you can't do it, and whoever brought it up to start with?"

⸺

A sign on a revival in the church read, "If not now, when? If not us, who? If not here, where?"

If there is one thing which pierces the Saviour's heart with unutterable grief, it is not the world's iniquity but the church's indifference. —F. B. Meyer.

One place where people seem to think they can get as much as ever for a quarter is in the church.

There are three crowds in every church: those who don't know what's happening, those who wonder what's happening, and those who make things happen.

GREAT CHURCHES ARE NOT BUILT WITH SPARE TIME AND POCKET CHANGE.

God puts the church in the world; Satan tries to put the world in the church.

Regarding the early church, someone said, "The prayers went up, the power came down, the people went out, the prospects came in, the preaching went on, and the persecution came." The same thing happened over and over again in the book of Acts.

Some people refuse to come up to the front of the church unless escorted by pallbearers.

⌐₥¬

Tell me what the young men of England are doing on Sunday and I will tell you what the future of England will be. —Gladstone.

⌐₥¬

THE DEVIL HAS NO GREAT INTEREST IN DESTROYING THE CHURCH; HE WOULD RATHER RUN IT.

⌐₥¬

It is true our Lord said, "Where two or three are gathered together there I'll be in the midst," but this does not necessarily mean that our Lord would not like to have a larger crowd. —Bob Jones, Sr.

⌐₥¬

A man proudly said: "I go to church only two times in my life— the first time they sprinkle water on me; the second time, they sprinkle rice." A hearer added: "And the third time, they sprinkle dirt."

⌐₥¬

EVERY TIME YOU WALK A MILE TO CHURCH AND CARRY A BIBLE, YOU PREACH A SERMON A MILE LONG —D. L. Moody.

⌐₥¬

What the church needs more than anything else is fewer people telling the church what it needs more than anything else.

⌐₥¬

A church that has to be supported by tea parties, ice cream socials and fried chicken is as weak as the tea, as cold as the ice cream and as dead as the chicken.

Most church members are 100% willing: 50% are willing to work, and the other 50% are willing to let them.

People do not miss church services because they live too far from the building; they miss because they live too far from God!

IF ABSENCE MAKES THE HEART GROW FONDER, THEN SOME PEOPLE MUST REALLY LOVE THEIR CHURCH!

The man who has not been to church for thirty years is usually the one who says that modern preaching is behind the times.

The church is the only organization in the world that attempts to fulfill its purpose with such a small percentage of its members involved. —C.W.H.

TWO DISTINGUISHING MARKS OF THE EARLY CHURCH WERE: (1) POVERTY; (2) POWER.

Confusion was created by a church bulletin which read: Text for today: "Thou Shalt Not Steal." The choir will sing, "Steal Away, Steal Away."

Anybody who thinks there is a shortage of coins hasn't been to church lately.

Comfort, Sorrow, Suffering

We can praise our Heavenly Father that sorrows and disappointments are not meant to disfigure but to transform us.

The rainbow of promise appears when the sunshine of His love meets the showers of our sorrow.

In the Bible, where human sorrows are most conspicuous, divine power was most compassionate. Mercy met misery on its own ground. —C.W.H.

There can be no meal without a mill, no throne without a thorn, no gain without pain, and no crown without a cross.

GOD OFTEN DIGS THE WELLS OF JOY WITH THE SPADE OF SORROW.

To ease another's heartache is to forget one's own. —Abraham Lincoln.

The soul would have no rainbow had the eyes no tears.

A SMOOTH SEA NEVER MADE A SKILLFUL SAILOR.

Never fear to suffer; but, oh, fear to sin! If you must choose between them, prefer the greatest suffering to the smallest
sin. —Guthrie.

To realize the worth of the anchor we need to feel the storm.

IF GOD SENDS THE STORM, HE WILL ALSO STEER THE VESSEL.

No affliction would trouble the child of God if he knew God's
reason for sending it.

*If each hung up his pack of troubles on a wall and looked around
at the troubles of others, he would quickly run to grab his
own.*

WHEN IT GETS DARK ENOUGH, THE STARS ALWAYS COME
OUT.

Suffering never stops at suffering. It comes out as wisdom,
tenderness, refinement and sympathy.

The cause, not the pain, makes the martyr.

Consecration, Dedication, Surrender

You are only valuable to God as you are available to God. —C.W.H.

.mm.

He is no fool who gives what he cannot keep, to gain what he cannot lose.

.mm.

As long as you are something, God is not everything; but when you are nothing, Christ is all. —C.W.H.

.mm.

THE LORD DOES NOT USE BORROWED VESSELS. —C.W.H.

.mm.

You may not be much but you can be faithful. —Lee Roberson.

.mm.

The biggest cemetery in the country is where unused talents are buried.

.mm.

Some have ability without consecration, while others have consecration without ability. Thank God for consecrated ability! —Bob Jones, Sr.

.mm.

Surrender is signing your name at the bottom of a blank sheet of paper and allowing God to fill in all the details. —C.W.H.

.mm.

Give God your heart and He will comb the kinks out of your head. —Bob Jones, Sr.

THE MAN WHO WALKS WITH GOD ALWAYS REACHES HIS DESTINATION. —C.W.H.

I'd rather have 10 fanatics than 10,000 placid followers. —Lenin (one of the fathers of communism).

I will place no value on anything I have or may possess, save in its relation to the kingdom of God. —David Livingstone.

God is no respecter of persons, but He is a great respecter of surrender. —Jesse Hendley.

ONE'S HANDS CAN ONLY BE FILLED WHEN THEY ARE OPEN.

"I would give the world to be as happy as you are," said someone to a happy Christian. "That's what it cost me," he replied.

When one lady was asked to dedicate her life to God, she replied: "Oh, no! I am miserable enough with what religion I now have. Please don't ask me to get any more."

Movements start, not with masses, but with individuals.

The real tragedy of life is not in being limited to one talent, but in the failure to use the one talent.

⌐oo¬

THE MAN WHO LOOKS BACK SOONER OR LATER GOES BACK.

⌐oo¬

I believe Jesus would demand today as close a following, as much suffering, as great self-denial, as when He lived in person on the earth and said, "Whosoever he be of you that forsaketh not all that he hath, he cannot be my disciple" (Luke 14:33).

⌐oo¬

WHAT'S MINE IS NOT MINE BUT GOD'S.

⌐oo¬

To obtain God's best, we must give our best—to win, we must surrender—to live, we must die—to receive, we must give. — Oswald J. Smith.

Convictions

If you don't stand for something, you will fall for anything.

⌐oo¬

There are things I would die for, there are things I would fight for that I would not die for, and still others I would fuss about that I would not fight over.

⌐oo¬

A fanatic is one who can't change his mind and won't change the subject. —Winston Churchill.

What a man accomplishes depends on what he believes. —*Banker Bulletin.*

Cowardice asks, "Is it safe?" Expediency asks, "Is it politic?" Vanity asks, "Is it popular?" But Conscience asks, "Is it right?" —Wm. Morley Punshon.

You can't be for something without being against something. You can't love flowers without hating weeds. —C.W.H.

When Martin Luther was told, "Mr. Luther, the whole world is against you," he calmly replied, "Then I'm against the whole world."

CONVICTIONS ARE SPARK PLUGS FOR ACTION.

Courtship, Marriage

Every bride and groom would do well to remember that, in "wedding," the "we" comes before the "I."

Marriage is an institution where a man loses his bachelor's degree and the lady gains her masters.

⌐⌐⌐

Some psychologists say girls tend to marry a man like their fathers. That may explain why so many mothers cry at weddings.

⌐⌐⌐

Many a girl who thinks she was bitten by the lovebug discovers it was only a louse.

⌐⌐⌐

If you keep doing after you get married what you did before you got married in order to get married, you won't ever get unmarried.

⌐⌐⌐

An optimist is an unmarried pessimist and a pessimist is a married optimist.

⌐⌐⌐

An old farmer, when asked why he had never married, explained: "Well, I'd rather go through life wanting something I didn't have, than having something I didn't want."

⌐⌐⌐

TO MARRY A WOMAN FOR HER BEAUTY IS LIKE BUYING A HOUSE FOR ITS PAINT.

⌐⌐⌐

Weddings have become so costly that it is now the father of the bride who breaks down and weeps.

⌐⌐⌐

A couple stood before the preacher to be married. The boy's hair was as long as the girl's. It was difficult to tell the two apart. So the minister said, "Whichever one you are, take whichever one this is, to be whatever you are going to be."

⌐▥⌐

Sign on the door of a marriage license bureau: OUT TO LUNCH—THINK IT OVER.

Determination

No situation in life can master you until you yourself pull down your flag. —James G. Gilkey.

⌐▥⌐

By perseverance the snail reached the ark. —Spurgeon.

⌐▥⌐

One of Andrew Jackson's boyhood friends said, "I could throw Andrew nine times out of ten, but he wouldn't stay throwed."

⌐▥⌐

To the timid and hesitating, everything is impossible because it seems so. —Sir Walter Scott.

⌐▥⌐

The men who have moved the world have been men whom the world could not move.

⌐▥⌐

I WILL GO ANYWHERE, PROVIDED IT BE FORWARD. —David
Livingstone.

One day Michelangelo saw a block of marble which the owner
said was of no value. "It is valuable to me," said
Michelangelo. "There is an angel imprisoned in it and I must
set it free."

*It is not your aptitude but your attitude that determines your
altitude.*

If you think you can, you're right; if you think you can't you're
right again. You won't be able to. For as a man thinketh
in his heart, so is he. —Henry Ford.

*IMPOSSIBLE is a word found only in the dictionary of
fools.* —Napoleon.

A man is a hero, not because he is braver than anyone else, but
because he is brave for ten minutes longer. —Emerson.

Devil, Satan

Satan is to be avoided as a lion; dreaded as a serpent; but he
must be feared as "an angel of light"!

The Devil did not tempt Adam and Eve to steal, to lie, to kill, to commit adultery; he tempted them to live independent of God. —Bob Jones, Sr.

Satan can build a wall around us, and often does, but he can never put a lid on it. So KEEP LOOKING UP!

Why, the very spelling of the Devil's name shows what he is— Devil, evil, vile, ill, hell! —Spurgeon.

The Devil doesn't try to get you to do a wrong thing. Rather, he tries to get you to do a right thing in the wrong way. —C.W.H.

THE DEVIL IS AN ARTIST. HE PAINTS SIN IN VERY ATTRACTIVE COLORS.

Discouragement

When we start thinking of defeat, too often the Devil has the victory already. —Jess Kauffman.

Ten rules for getting rid of the blues: go out and do something for someone else and repeat it nine times.

DON'T YOU GET TIRED OF SWINGING THE AX HANDLE WITH NO HEAD ON IT? —C.W.H.

Education, Wisdom, Knowledge

There is no tragedy as tragic as combining high mentality with low morality. —Bob Jones, Sr.

Everybody is ignorant, only on different subjects. —Will Rogers.

Never get mad at anyone for knowing more than you do; it isn't his fault.

WISDOM IS THE ABILITY TO USE KNOWLEDGE SUCCESS-FULLY. —C.W.H.

The man who doesn't read good books has no advantage over the man who can't read them.

We should be as careful of the books we read as of the company we keep.

You should have education enough so you won't have to look

up to people; and then more education so you will be wise enough not to look down on people. —M. L. Boren.

_~mn~_

There is no time in life when books do not influence a man. — Walter Besant.

_~mn~_

A college education never hurt anybody who was willing to learn something afterwards.

_~mn~_

College is a place where nonconformists conform to the prevailing standard of nonconformity.

_~mn~_

Someone said to Helen Keller, "What a pity you have no sight!" to which she replied, "Yes, but what a pity so many have sight but cannot see!"

_~mn~_

The three *R's* used to be Reading, 'Ritin' and 'Rithmetic. Today they are Rioting, Rebellion and Restlessness. If this continues, we will have Regret, Rot and Ruin. What we need is Respect, Religion and Responsibility. —Dr. Whitt N. Schultz.

_~mn~_

Experience may not be worth what it costs, but I can't seem to get it for any less. —Presbyterian Life.

_~mn~_

I'd rather hear a man say, "I seen," when he has seen something, than to hear a man say, "I have seen," when he ain't seen nothing. —Bob Jones, Sr.

_~mn~_

You can get knowledge from reading books or attending college, but wisdom comes from God. —C.W.H.

Education is not salvation. If you educate a thief, you only make him a more successful and crafty thief.

Addressing a group of the brightest high school students in America, Henry Ford once said, "There is no such thing as no chance."

Talk and you say what you already know; but listen and you learn something new.

Education is the development of all one's ordinary powers to an extraordinary degree of efficiency. —Theodore Roosevelt.

IT IS IMPOSSIBLE TO MAKE WISDOM HEREDITARY.

Dr. R. G. Lee said to a man who refused to accept the Genesis account of creation, "You have gagged on a rib and swallowed a monkey, and you call that scholarship!"

Personally I am always ready to learn, although I do not always like being taught. —Winston Churchill.

YOU DON'T HAVE TO BE LISTED IN "WHO'S WHO" TO KNOW WHAT'S WHAT.

Knowledge is one thing that doesn't become secondhand when used.

Said the girl graduate, "Four years of college—and whom has it gotten me?"—She evidently went to get her "M-R-S." degree.

I always go to the right source for advice. I would not ask a man on Broadway in New York who says, "opossum" how to catch "possums." I would ask a fellow from the country who owns a cur dog and who says "possum." —Bob Jones, Sr.

EDUCATION WITHOUT SALVATION LEADS TO RUINATION.

Experience is a good teacher, but a hard one. She gives the test first and the lesson afterward.

You can't no more learn somethin' from anyone who don't know nothin' that you can come back from anywhere you ain't been.

One cannot follow his conscience unless his conscience has been properly educated. An uneducated conscience is a dangerous guide. —C.W.H.

Why can't life's problems hit us when we're 18 and know all the answers?

Reading maketh a full man; conference maketh a ready man; and writing maketh an accurate man.

⌐ⵑ⌐

One college freshman was so dumb that he stayed up all night studying for a blood test.

⌐ⵑ⌐

The only ignorance that is bliss is the ignorance of the man who thinks he knows it all. —C.W.H.

Eternity—Heaven, Hell, Death

Don't sacrifice the permanent on the altar of the immediate. — Bob Jones, Sr.

⌐ⵑ⌐

Christians never meet for the last time.

⌐ⵑ⌐

No one is so old that he cannot live yet another year, nor so young that he cannot die today.

⌐ⵑ⌐

ETERNITY NEVER GROWS OLDER.

⌐ⵑ⌐

Living is death; dying is life. On this side of the grave we are exiles; on that, citizens; on this side, orphans; on that, children; on this side, captives; on that, free men; on this, disguised, unknown; on that, disclosed and proclaimed as the sons of God. —Henry Ward Beecher.

⌐₥⌐

My interest is in the future because I am going to spend the rest of my life there. —Charles F. Kettering.

⌐₥⌐

In just a few years memory's house is all we will have to live in.

⌐₥⌐

IT DOES NOT REQUIRE A DECISION TO GO TO HELL.

⌐₥⌐

Anything you have because of what Christ did for you, you cannot lose. But anything you have because of what you did for Christ can be lost.

⌐₥⌐

A man is a fool who thinks, because he does not believe in Hell, that his opinion shuts the door and puts out the fire. —Billy Sunday.

⌐₥⌐

One evangelist said, "First you have a man, then a movement, then a monument."

⌐₥⌐

Take care of your life and the Lord will take care of your death. — George Whitefield.

⌐₥⌐

A PERSON NEVER GETS TOO BUSY TO ATTEND HIS OWN FUNERAL.

⌐₥⌐

The undertaker is the only person in the world who always puts the customer in his place.

~~~

When Bishop George Brunk had preached on the infidelity of persons like Robert Ingersoll, a brother came to him wondering whether it was all right to buy Ingersoll watches. The Bishop smiled and said, "Certainly. Ingersoll will do for time, but not for eternity."

~~~

THE ROAD TO HELL IS PAVED WITH GOOD INTENTIONS.

~~~

An epitaph is a belated advertisement for a line of goods that has been permanently discontinued.

~~~

No dying person has ever said, "I'm sorry I was a Christian."

~~~

THE WISE MAN ALWAYS PREPARES FOR THE INEVITABLE. —
Bob Jones, Sr.

~~~

Death is not extinguishing the light from the Christian; it is putting out the lamp because the dawn has come.

~~~

A man is never ready to live until he is ready to die.

~~~

Life is a one-way street and we are not coming back.

~~~

A man can slip into Hell with his hand on the doorknob of Heaven. —Billy Sunday.

⌐m⌐

Judging from the general behavior we see in this world nowadays, Hell must be experiencing a population explosion, too.

⌐m⌐

LIFE WITH CHRIST IS AN ENDLESS HOPE: WITHOUT HIM, A HOPELESS END.

⌐m⌐

Is your passport for eternity in order? Do not neglect; you may need it sooner than you think.

⌐m⌐

Science has brought longer life but has not conquered death.

⌐m⌐

HELL IS TRUTH SEEN TOO LATE —H. G. Adams.

Excuses

Our inability is never an excuse when God gives the command. —Fisher.

⌐m⌐

THE ONLY THING WORSE THAN FAILURE IS TRYING TO EXCUSE IT. —C.W.H.

⌐m⌐

Feeding your conscience excuses is like feeding your watchdog sleeping pills.

⌐ɰɰ¬

Ninety-nine percent of the failures come from people who have the habit of making excuses. —George Washington Carver.

⌐ɰɰ¬

IF YOU HAVE A GOOD EXCUSE, DON'T USE IT.

Faith, Trust

Mr. Moody's favorite verse was, "I will trust and not be afraid." He used to say, "You can travel to Heaven first-class or second-class. First-class is, 'I will trust and not be afraid.' Second-class is, 'What time I am afraid, I will trust in thee.'"

⌐ɰɰ¬

Faith is to believe what we do not see, and the reward of this faith is to see what we believe.

⌐ɰɰ¬

FAITH STEPS UPON THE SEEMING VOID AND FINDS THE ROCK BENEATH.

⌐ɰɰ¬

You will never learn faith in comfortable surroundings. —A. B. Simpson.

⌐ɰɰ¬

The world says, "Show me and I'll believe you!" Christ says, "Believe Me and I'll show you!"

We may not always be able to trace God, but we can always trust Him.

Faith knows that whenever she gets a black envelope from the heavenly post office, there is a treasure in it. —Spurgeon.

We may not always be able to trace God, but we can always trust Him.

WHERE GOD HAS PUT A PERIOD, DON'T CHANGE IT TO A QUESTION MARK.

I believe the promises of God enough to venture an eternity on them. —G. Campbell Morgan.

He who knows the way of the Lord can find it in the dark.

Faith is the daring of the soul to go farther than it can see.

God will not send the winds to drive our ship of salvation unless we have faith to lift the sails. —Billy Sunday.

It is impossible for Faith to overdraw its account in God's bank.

Faith is telling a mountain to move and being shocked only if it doesn't.

WHEN GOD BOLTS A DOOR, DON'T TRY TO GET THROUGH A
WINDOW.

Faith goes up the stairs that love has made and looks out of the
window which hope has opened. —Spurgeon.

When faith goes to market, he always takes his basket.

You can take a little faith and get a great big Saviour. It is not
the measure of faith but the object of faith that saves (John
3:36). —C.W.H.

*He who is small in faith will never be great in anything but
failure.*

Stranger: "Are you the little woman of great faith?" *Woman:*
"No, I'm the woman of little faith in the great God."

FAITH WILL NOT MAKE THE SUN RISE SOONER, BUT IT WILL
MAKE THE NIGHT SEEM SHORTER.

Only he who can see the invisible can do the impossible. —Frank
Gaines.

Fear

It has been said that our anxiety does not empty tomorrow of its sorrows, but only empties today of its strength.

FEAR NOT TOMORROW; GOD IS ALREADY THERE.

Into the granite that marks the grave of one of America's greatest astronomers are carved these words: "I have lived too long among the stars to fear the night."

If you fear that people will know, don't do it.

Friends, Enemies

When we lose a friend, we die a little.

It is smart to pick your friends—but not to pieces.

A man who has no enemies is no good. You cannot move without producing friction. —Bob Jones, Sr.

PROSPERITY BEGETS FRIENDS; ADVERSITY REVEALS THEM.

Together the links make the chain, together the shingles make the roof, together the bricks make the wall, united we stand, divided we fall. —R. G. Lee.

If you were another person, would you like to be a friend of yours?

When you measure your friends, do you use a microscope for discovering their virtues and a magnifying glass for examining their faults?

SHORT VISITS MAKE LONG FRIENDS.

Associate with men of good quality if you esteem your own reputation, for it is better to be alone than in bad company. —George Washington.

The way to destroy an enemy is to make him your friend.

Be friendly with the people you know. If it were not for them, you would be a total stranger.

During a tough time in life, someone said to me, "You've lost a friend, haven't you?" And I replied, "No, I've simply discovered an enemy. If he were my friend, he would still be my friend." —C.W.H.

We are on the wrong track when we think of friendship as something to get rather than something to give.

Sometimes it seems like friends come and go but not so with enemies; they accumulate.

Every friend lost pushes you one step closer to the brink of character bankruptcy.

The enemies you make by taking a strong stand have more respect for you than the friends you make by straddling the fence.

Having common enemies is a poor basis for fellowship. —C.W.H.

FRIENDS LAST LONGER THE LESS THEY ARE USED.

If you really want to know who your friends are, just make a mistake.

A friend is a present you give to yourself.

THERE IS NO HARMONY WHEN YOU SING ALONE.

Giving

Give God all He asks, and receive all He promises.

Giving until it hurts is not a true measure of charity. Some are more easily hurt than others.

"The liberal soul shall be made fat" (Prov. 11:25). Such was Hannah's experience. She gave away one child, and God paid her back with five. —Guthrie.

We make a living by what we get; but we make a life by what we give. —Winston Churchill.

Giving to the Lord is but transporting our goods to a higher floor.

WHEN IT COMES TO GIVING, SOME PEOPLE STOP AT NOTHING.

No person was ever honored for what he received. Honor has been the reward for what he gave. —Calvin Coolidge.

God sees the heart, not the hand; the giver, not the gift.

⌐ᴍᴍ⌐

HE WHO GIVES ONLY WHEN HE IS ASKED HAS WAITED TOO
LONG.

⌐ᴍᴍ⌐

You can't get enough from God to leave Him with any less than
He had when He started giving. —C.W.H.

Gossip, Criticism

It has been suggested that, if you are not big enough to stand
criticism, you are too small to be praised.

⌐ᴍᴍ⌐

*When you bury the hatchet, make sure it is not in your neighbor's
head.*

⌐ᴍᴍ⌐

He who tells the faults of others to you will probably tell yours
to the other fellow at his first opportunity.

⌐ᴍᴍ⌐

THE EASIEST THING ON EARTH TO FIND IS FAULT.

⌐ᴍᴍ⌐

*People cannot be judged by what others say about them, but they
can be judged by what they say about others.*

⌐ᴍᴍ⌐

Constructive criticism is that which is accompanied by
    solitude, tenderness, and prayer. Destructive criticism is
    that which is accompanied by harshness, bitterness,
    jealousy, and pride.

*Spreading gossip is impossible if we refuse to listen—or to believe
    it.*

You can't throw mud at others without getting your own hands
    dirty.

*People and telephones repeat what they hear, but the telephone
    repeats it exactly.*

UNSOLICITED ADVICE IS A FORM OF CRITICISM. —C.W.H.

A lie will travel around the world twice while truth is still get-
    ting his boots on. —Will Rogers.

When you are throwing mud, you are losing ground.

Do right a thousand times, and you may not hear of it once; do
    wrong once, and you will hear of it a thousand times.

People will believe anything if you whisper it.

If criticizing gives you pain, then do it; if it gives you the slightest pleasure, then keep your mouth shut.

THERE ARE NO IDLE RUMORS. RUMORS ARE ALWAYS BUSY.

Never fear criticism when you are right; never ignore criticism when you are wrong.

Wise people believe only half of what they hear. Wiser ones know which half to believe. —Alexander Pope.

Constructive criticism is when I criticize you; destructive criticism is when you criticize me.

Even a tombstone will say good things about a fellow when he is down.

One tree can make a million matches; but one match can destroy a million trees.

NOTHING IS DIRT CHEAP ANYMORE EXCEPT GOSSIP.

Some people have as their motto: "If you can't say anything good about a person, let's hear it."

Government, America, Patriotism, War

The strength of a country is the strength of its religious convictions. —Calvin Coolidge.

WHAT THIS COUNTRY NEEDS IS DIRTIER FINGERNAILS AND CLEANER MINDS. —Will Rogers.

The policy of the American government is to leave their citizens free: neither restraining nor aiding in their pursuits. — Thomas Jefferson.

There is not a man in the country who can't make a living for himself and family, but he can't make a living for them and his government, too, the way his government is living. What the government has got to do is live as cheap as the people do. —Will Rogers.

True patriotism should make the heart beat faster and the tongue wag slower.

Why is it that the liberals, who act so shocked at the idea of capital punishment for criminals, are so active in campaigning for the slaughter of the innocent by abortion? —News and Notes.

A POLITICIAN THINKS OF THE NEXT ELECTION. A STATESMAN
THINKS OF THE NEXT GENERATION.

⌐␣␣⌐

Alexander Hamilton started the U. S. Treasury with nothing,
and that was the closest our country has ever been to being
even. —Will Rogers.

⌐␣␣⌐

*Maybe we should put the designers of women's bathing suits in
charge of the federal budget.*

⌐␣␣⌐

If freedom is right and tyranny is wrong, why should those who
believe in freedom treat it as if it were a roll of bologna to
be bought a slice at a time? —Senator Jesse Helms.

⌐␣␣⌐

*No man is good enough to govern another man without the other's
consent.* —Abraham Lincoln.

⌐␣␣⌐

Isn't it remarkable how our pioneering ancestors built up a great
nation without asking Congress for help?

⌐␣␣⌐

*True patriotism is our conviction that this country is superior to
all others because we were born in it.*

⌐␣␣⌐

A man who will not use his freedom to defend his freedom does
not deserve his freedom. —Carl McIntire.

⌐␣␣⌐

CRIME'S STORY WOULD LIKELY BE SHORTER IF THE SENTENCES WERE LONGER.

We deserve liberty only so long as we are willing to sacrifice for it. —Benjamin Franklin.

Any government big enough to give you everything you want, is big enough to take away everything you have. —Gerald Ford.

If you make any money, the government shoves you in the creek once a year with it in your pockets, and all that don't get wet you can keep. —Will Rogers.

PATRIOTISM HAS NOT DISCHARGED ITS FULL DUTY WHEN IT HANGS OUT A FLAG.

It used to be that when you said a man had gone to his everlasting rest, it didn't mean he had landed a job with the government.

All murder is killing, but not all killing is murder. God not only condones, He commands capital punishment. —C.W.H.

A lot of people believe in law and order as long as they can lay down the law and give the orders.

PEACE AND FREEDOM NEVER COME AT BARGAIN PRICES.

The future of our country depends upon the Christian training of our youth. —George Washington.

⌐ɯɯ⌐

If and when American civilization collapses, historians of a future date can look back and sneer, "They entertained themselves to death." —Jim Frankel.

⌐ɯɯ⌐

MERCY TO THE CRIMINAL IS CRUELTY TO THE COMMUNITY. —C.W.H.

⌐ɯɯ⌐

In the span of something like three quarters of a century this country has gone from the little red schoolhouse to the big consolidated schoolhouse in the red.

⌐ɯɯ⌐

In the last four thousand years of history, there have been but 268 years entirely free of war. —Coronet.

⌐ɯɯ⌐

One has to be very careful with political jokes because many times political jokes get elected.

⌐ɯɯ⌐

Income tax has made more liars out of the American people than golf. —Will Rogers.

⌐ɯɯ⌐

If inflation gets much worse, it will soon be an insult to tell a girl she looks like a million dollars! —Wendell Kent.

⌐ɯɯ⌐

The death penalty may not eliminate crime, but it stops repeaters.

America has more food to eat than any other country in the world, and more diets to keep us from eating it!

Habits

A conscious act performed often enough becomes an unconscious habit. —C.W.H.

The chains of habit are generally too small to be felt until they are too strong to be broken.

WE FIRST MAKE OUR HABITS, THEN OUR HABITS MAKE US.

Someone has said that profanity is the effort of a feeble mind to express itself forcibly.

Stout matron to friend: "I only weigh myself on days when everything goes wrong. I figure those days are ruined anyway." —Franklin Folger.

THE BEST WAY TO BREAK A HABIT IS TO DROP IT.

One man who couldn't lose weight no matter what he tried, said to a friend, "I would get fat on embalming fluid!"

Having listened to more profanity than he could endure, a man turned to the swearer and asked, "How much does Satan pay you for such profanity?" When told he received nothing, the man continued: "You certainly work cheap for a thing which destroys character and makes you less than a gentleman."

CANCER, A CURE FOR SMOKING.

No one should try to do two things at once, and this includes women who put on weight and slacks at the same time.

The doctor said to his overweight patient, "Follow this diet and in a couple of months I want to see three-fourths of you back in my office for a checkup."

One way to lose weight is to eat all you want of everything you don't like.

Cursing is the only sin that the Devil gets us to commit without giving us anything for it. —John R. Rice.

HE WHO GAMBLES PICKS HIS OWN POCKET.

_،mm.,_

As kids, some started smoking cigarettes because they thought it was smart. Why don't they stop for the same reason?

Happiness, Joy, Laughter

If you have no joy in your religion, there's a leak in your Christianity somewhere. —Billy Sunday.

_،mm.,_

A smile can add a great deal to one's face value.

_،mm.,_

THOSE WHO WISH TO SING ALWAYS FIND A SONG.

_،mm.,_

The road to happiness is forever under construction. —Thomas Jefferson.

_،mm.,_

A person who can smile when things go wrong has probably just thought of someone he can blame.

_،mm.,_

If we are good Christians, it should take little to make us happy and much to make us unhappy.

_،mm.,_

Somebody said j-o-y—joy: J for Jesus, Y for you; nothing between Jesus and you spells J-o-y.

Before we set our hearts too much upon anything, let us examine how happy they are who already possess it.

When someone once asked William Booth his great secret to happiness, he replied, "I never say no to the Lord."

If I knew there was no Hell, I would still want my children to be saved just for the peace and happiness it brings in this life. —C.W.H.

Happiness in some cases should be spelled "happen-ness" because it depends on what happens.

A smile is the most important thing one can wear!

Humor is the hole that lets the sawdust out of a stuffed shirt.

HAPPINESS IS THE CHILD OF OBEDIENCE. —C.W.H.

Both cheerfulness and grumbling are contagious. It's up to you what kind of an epidemic you start.

A genuine sense of humor is the pole that adds balance to our steps as we walk the tightrope of life.

True happiness may be sought, thought, or caught—but never bought.

LAUGHTER IS A TRANQUILIZER WITH NO SIDE EFFECTS.

Happiness is not perfected until shared with others.

I have learned to seek my happiness by limiting my desires, rather than in attempting to satisfy them. —John Stuart Mill.

The secret of happiness is not to do what you like, but to like what you do.

LAUGHTER HAS NO FOREIGN ACCENT.

One nice thing about being imperfect is the joy that it brings to others.

Happiness comes not from having much to live on but from having much to live for.

People all over the world smile in the same language.

It takes 72 muscles to frown—only 14 to smile!

Keep smiling: it makes everyone wonder what you are up to.

Holy Spirit

Before a Christian is Spirit-filled, it is hard to do an easy task; but after he is Spirit-filled, it is easy to do a hard task.

Although a Christian can never lose the precious gift of salvation, he can still have a power failure.

C. H. MacIntosh once said, "Let us bear in mind that where the Holy Ghost is working, one instrument is as good and as efficient as seventy; and where He is not working, seventy are of no more value than one."

I was afraid to talk about the Spirit-filled life; I was so afraid I would get out on a limb that I never bothered to climb the tree. —C.W.H.

Home—Father, Mother, Children

Parents wonder why the streams are bitter when they themselves have poisoned the fountain.

The reason some men don't bring the boss home for dinner is that she is already there.

The warmth of a home is not necessarily determined by its heating system.

The child who does not obey father and mother will obey neither social, civil, moral, nor Divine laws. —L. E. Maxwell.

A house is not a home; it is a place to put your home. —C.W.H.

The best way to get rid of criminals is to stop raising them. — John R. Rice.

Many marriages would work out better if both sides would operate on a thrifty-thrifty basis.

The home can be the strongest ally of the Sunday school or its greatest enemy, depending on the parents.

One of the best things a father can do for his children is to demonstrate an obvious love for their mother.

Behind every successful man there is a wife with a hard-working husband.

Children are a great comfort in your old age—and they help you reach it faster, too.

If you treat your wife like a thoroughbred, she won't turn out to be a nag.

In the old days a naughty child was straightened up by being bent over. —*Farmers' Almanac.*

Children disgrace us in public by behaving just like we do at home.

Speaking to the marriage counselor, the woman said, "That's my side of the story—now let me tell you his."

CHILDREN, LIKE CANOES, BEHAVE BETTER IF PADDLED FROM THE REAR.

What should not be heard by little ears should not be said by big mouths.

Story entitled "The Generations": grandfather had a farm; father a garden; son a can opener.

If you don't want your children to hear what you're saying, pretend you're talking to them.

What shall it profit a man if he should gain the whole world and lose his own children?

Small boys are washable, but most of them shrink from it.

CHILDREN ARE HAPPIER WHEN PARENTS REQUIRE OBEDIENCE.

Juvenile delinquency was unheard of many years ago because the problem was thrashed out in the woodshed.

Once truth is firmly planted in a child, it continues steadfast through any test; but the planting has to be done early in the growing season. —Marcelene Cox.

Television is an appliance which changes children from irresistible forces into immovable objects. —Philadelphia Principal.

The death of a mother is the first sorrow wept without her.

When a frazzled mother sent her little boy to bed, she heard him grumbling to himself, "Every time she gets tired, it's me that has to take a nap." —Cleon Lyles.

A child who does not hear about religion at his mother's knee is not likely to hear about it at any other joint.

"If at first you don't succeed," the modern child psychologist advised the youngster, "cry, cry again."

IT NOW COSTS MORE TO AMUSE A CHILD THAN IT ONCE DID TO EDUCATE HIS FATHER.

The greatest danger confronting the children today is the example set by adults.

There was a time when parents taught their children the value of a dollar. Today they try to keep the bad news from them as long as possible.

It's hard to believe those involved in a divorce suit are the same people who were married.

It took the old-time mother less than a minute to dress for dinner because all she had to do was take off her apron.

A SWITCH IN TIME SAVES CRIME.

Visiting a family where the father had just died, the preacher asked the young son, "What were your father's last words?" "He didn't have any," said the boy, "Mama was with him to the end."

⌐▥⌐

THE BEST THING TO SPEND ON YOUR CHILDREN IS YOUR TIME.

⌐▥⌐

We should begin with the high chair instead of the electric chair in our efforts to check crime.

⌐▥⌐

Some women work so hard to make good husbands that they never quite manage to make good wives.

⌐▥⌐

Discipline doesn't break a child's spirit half as often as the lack of it breaks a parent's heart.

⌐▥⌐

A house is made of walls and beams; a home is built with love and dreams.

⌐▥⌐

All Hell cannot tear a boy or girl away from a praying mother. — Billy Sunday.

⌐▥⌐

A BOY IS THE ONLY THING GOD CAN USE TO MAKE A MAN.

⌐▥⌐

A father of ten was asked why he had so many children. "Because," he said, "we never wanted the youngest one to be spoiled!"

⌐▥⌐

A mother is the only person on earth who can divide her love among ten children and each child still have all her love.

⸺

Every father should remember that one day his children may follow his example instead of his advice.

⸺

Two long-haired teenage sons gave their father a surprise birthday gift—a box filled with their sheared locks and a card which read: "Dear Dad: Forgive us our past tresses." — *Detroit Free Press.*

⸺

All men are born free, but some get married. —E. C. McKenzie.

⸺

It's a happy home where the only scraps are those brushed off the dining table.

⸺

A mother said to her children, "Mind your manners; they may come back in style someday."

⸺

Today's unchurched child is tomorrow's criminal. —J. Edgar Hoover.

⸺

Statistics show that men who kiss their wives goodbye in the morning live five years longer than those who don't. So some of you men had better pucker up before you tucker out.

⸺

A BROKEN HOME IS THE WORLD'S GREATEST WRECK.

⸺

Every family tree has some sap in it.

As one boy said, "I was thinking all these horrible thoughts about my parents when suddenly it hit me: If they're all that bad, how come I'm so wonderful?"

We've got kids who have not yet sprouted long breeches, who know more about sin and vice than Methuselah. —Billy Sunday.

In our modern society, we run everything in the house with a switch except our children.

Face powder may catch a man, but it takes baking powder to hold him.

A FAMILY ALTAR WOULD ALTER MANY A FAMILY.

To keep a small boy out of the cookie jar, lock it and hide the key under a cake of soap.

Adam and Eve had an ideal marriage: he didn't have to hear about all the men she could have married; she didn't have to hear about the ways his mother cooked it.

It is not easy to straighten in the oak the crook that grew in the sapling. —Gaelic.

A thoughtful husband is one who remembers his wife's birthday but forgets which one it is.

The way to keep some teenage girls out of hot water is to put dirty dishes in it.

All she knows about cooking is how to bring a man to a boil.

Good marriages are not the result of finding the right person but being the right person.

The Hollywood version of the famous quotation seems to be, "Thou shalt love one, another, and another, and another."

Honesty

Honesty is still the best policy, but some people are satisfied with less than the best.

A man should never be ashamed to own that he has been in the wrong, which is but saying he is wiser today than he was yesterday. —Jonathan Swift.

It pays to be honest. But a man who is honest because it pays is not really honest; he is greedy. —C.W.H.

⌐𝓂𝓂⌐

Live so your autograph will be wanted, not your fingerprints.

Humility

Great men can lower themselves to fellowship with people on almost any level, but a man who only thinks he's great cannot come down to his own level. —C.W.H.

⌐𝓂𝓂⌐

Pride is the most peculiar disease known to the human family; it makes everyone sick except the fellow who has it.

⌐𝓂𝓂⌐

THE SMALLER WE BECOME, THE MORE ROOM GOD HAS TO WORK.

⌐𝓂𝓂⌐

A man can counterfeit hope and all other graces, but it is very difficult to counterfeit humility. —D. L. Moody.

⌐𝓂𝓂⌐

Humility is the strange thing one loses the moment he thinks he has it.

⌐𝓂𝓂⌐

Pride is the stone over which many people stumble. —Bob Jones, Sr.

A young man who had just received his degree from college rushed out and said, "Here I am, world; I have my A.B." Someone replied, "Sit down, son, and I'll teach you the rest of the alphabet."

Beware of the man who "kowtows" to his superiors or is rude to his inferiors. —Bob Jones, Sr.

NO GARMENT IS MORE BECOMING TO A CHRISTIAN THAN THE CLOAK OF HUMILITY.

When a man starts singing his own praises, it is pretty sure to be a solo.

The man who humbly bows before God is sure to walk upright before men.

God sends no one away empty except those who are full of themselves —D. L. Moody.

An egotist is a man who believes that if he had never been born, everyone would wonder why. —Dick Mills.

When a man toots his own horn, he usually gets the pitch too high.

A proud man is seldom a grateful man because a proud man
thinks he never gets all he really deserves. —Henry Ward
Beecher.

The fellow who has a right to boast doesn't have to.

The strongest men in the world are those who are weak before
God; the greatest men are those who are humble before God;
the tallest men are those who bend before God. —Richard
Halverson.

*It is often surprising to find what heights may be obtained
merely by remaining on the level.*

The higher you rise in the likeness of Jesus, the lower you will
stoop in your service for others.

*Praise is like perfume—a little bit won't hurt you if you don't
swallow it!* —Benjamin Franklin.

You can always tell an egotist, but you can't tell him much.

A man with both feet on the ground hasn't far to fall.

DON'T EXPECT APPLAUSE...DESERVE IT!

The only time to look down on your neighbor is when you are bending over to help him.

⌐m⌐

When two egotists meet, it is a case of an "I" for an "I."

⌐m⌐

The horn blowing the loudest is the one in the fog.

⌐m⌐

Swallow your pride occasionally. It is nonfattening.

⌐m⌐

Always remember this: the soundest way to progress in any organization is to help the man ahead of you to get promoted. —L. S. Hamaker.

⌐m⌐

WHEN YOU THINK YOU HAVE HUMILITY, YOU'VE LOST IT!

⌐m⌐

There is no limit to what can be accomplished if it doesn't matter who gets the credit.

Influence

People take your example far more seriously than they do your advice.

⌐m⌐

A reputation once broken may possibly be repaired, but the world will always keep its eye on the spot where the crack was.

Everybody can give pleasure in some way. One person may do it by coming into a room, another, by going out.

No man is so insignificant as to be sure his example can do no hurt. —Lord Clarendon.

Everyone leaves footprints on the sands of time—some, the print of a great sole; and others, the mark of a heel.

People are instructed by our words, but they are inspired only by our example.

Someday—somewhere, I shall see what my life has come to mean to those who have watched me live. —Daniel B. Brose.

People judge you by three things: the way you look, the way you talk, and the way you act. And most judgments are based solely on your appearance since the majority of the people who see you never get to hear you talk nor observe your actions. —C.W.H.

Kindness

Speak kind words, and you will hear kind echoes.

It's nice to be important, but it's more important to be nice.

One can pay back the loan of gold, but one dies forever in debt to those who are kind. —Malayan Proverb.

Kindness is a language that the dumb can speak and the deaf can hear and understand.

THE GREATER THE MAN, THE GREATER THE COURTESY.

There is no better exercise for the heart than reaching down and lifting people up.

To handle yourself, use your head; to handle others, use your heart.

Be nice to everyone you pass on your way up; you may have to meet them again on your way down.

No one is too big to be courteous, but some are too small.

The way to a man's heart is not down his throat. —C.W.H.

Leadership

If God were to rewrite Hebrews 11, choosing men of today to replace the Old Testament leaders, would your name be chosen?

Everything rises or falls on leadership. —Lee Roberson.

To know how to say what others only know how to think is what makes men poets and sages; and to dare to say what others only dare to think makes men martyrs or reformers. — Elizabeth Charles.

He who would be great must be fervent in his prayers, fearless in his principles, firm in his purposes, and faithful in his promises.

The measure of a man's greatness is not how many people serve him, but how many people he serves. —C.W.H.

When God calls a leader, He always supplies followers. —C.W.H.

⌐▥⌐

I do not like the phrase, "Never cross a bridge until you come to it." The world is owned by men who crossed bridges in their imaginations miles and miles in advance of the procession. —Bruce Barton.

⌐▥⌐

THE MAN WHO FIDDLES AROUND SELDOM GETS TO LEAD THE ORCHESTRA. —E. C. McKenzie.

⌐▥⌐

Our vision must be like that of Christ, whose telescopic view took in the whole world, and whose microscopic insight included every individual.

⌐▥⌐

A good supervisor, someone once said, is a guy who can step on your toes without messing up your shine.

⌐▥⌐

Civilization is in danger when those who have never learned to obey are given the right to command.

⌐▥⌐

MEN WHO CONQUER GO IN FOR ATTACK. —Spurgeon.

Liquor

The tavernkeeper is the only businessman who is ashamed of his best customers.

⌐▥⌐

The liquor traffic would destroy the church if it could, and the church could destroy the liquor traffic if it would. —National Voice.

The tavernkeeper likes the drunkard, but he does not want him for a son-in-law.

All the umpires together have not put as many ballplayers out of the game as old man booze. —Connie Mack.

To put alcohol in the human body is like putting sand in the bearings of an engine. —Thomas A. Edison.

An elderly person asked her aged father, "Father, why did you never drink? Was it because you didn't like it?" "No," he replied, "it was because I did."

Whiskey is God's worst enemy and the Devil's best friend. — Billy Sunday.

Alcohol makes a man colorful: it gives him a red nose, a white liver, a yellow streak and a blue outlook.

Statistics show that 10,000 people are killed by liquor where only one is killed by a mad dog; yet we shoot the dog and license the liquor. What sense is there to this? —*Bible Crusaders News.*

A DRUNK IS THE PAST TENSE OF A DRINK.

There are no depths of cruelty or criminality in the history of the human race to which people have not descended when under the influence of liquor. —R. G. Lee.

Love, Forgiveness

A man may die and go to Hell unsaved, but he will never go to Hell unloved. —C.W.H.

The love that unites Christians is stronger than the differences that divide them.

God uses the thermometer of obedience to test the temperature of love. —Bob Jones, Jr.

LOVE ADDS AND SUBTRACTS BUT NEVER KEEPS SCORE.

A sign on the wall in a dentist's office: *People do not care how much you know until they know how much you care.*

Life is one fool thing after another, and love is two fool things
    after each other.

⌐ ▭ ⌐

Love does not keep a ledger of the sins and failures of others.

⌐ ▭ ⌐

When asked to define love, a little boy said, "Love is a feeling
    that you feel when you feel like you are going to feel a feel-
    ing that you have never felt before."

⌐ ▭ ⌐

Service can never become slavery to one who loves. —Massee.

⌐ ▭ ⌐

WHERE LOVE IS THIN, FAULTS ARE THICK.

⌐ ▭ ⌐

About Abraham Lincoln: "His heart was as great as the world,
    but there was no room in it to hold the memory of a wrong."

⌐ ▭ ⌐

Love your neighbor, yet don't pull down your hedge. —Benjamin
    Franklin.

⌐ ▭ ⌐

The heart that loves is always young.

⌐ ▭ ⌐

*A little boy, on being asked what forgiveness was, gave the an-
    swer, "It is the scent that flowers give when they are tram-
    pled on!"*

⌐ ▭ ⌐

When love and skill work together, expect a masterpiece. —John
    Ruskin.

⌐ ▭ ⌐

Of all human passions, love is the strongest, for it attacks simultaneously the head, the heart and the senses.

Money, Riches, Prosperity

It is dangerous when our yearning capacity becomes greater than our earning capacity.

Our ancestors had to haul the washwater from the well, but they didn't have to sit up nights figuring out how to meet the payments on the bucket.

John Wesley once said: "Make all you can and give all you can."

I have heard a group of poor people sing, "I'm satisfied with Jesus," but I've never heard a group of millionaires sing, "I'm satisfied with money." —C.W.H.

BUY NOT SILK WHEN YOU OWE FOR MILK.

It's good to have money and the things money can buy, but it's good, too, to check up once in a while to make sure you haven't lost the things that money can't buy. —George H. Lorimer.

⌐▥⌐

Bein' poor is a problem, but bein' rich ain't the answer. —
C. Grant.

⌐▥⌐

What we do with what we have is more important than what we have. —C.W.H.

⌐▥⌐

One out of every six verses in the New Testament mentions the right or wrong use of possessions.

⌐▥⌐

In the world it is not what we take up, but what we give up, that makes us rich. —Henry Ward Beecher.

⌐▥⌐

Today the average philosophy is, "Make all you can, can all you make, sit on the can, and poison the rest."

⌐▥⌐

NO MAN IS RICH ENOUGH TO BUY BACK HIS PAST. — Oscar Wilde.

⌐▥⌐

Golf is a lot like taxes—you drive hard to get to the green and then wind up in the hole.

⌐▥⌐

We live in a day and age when we know the price tag of nearly everything but the value of hardly anything.

⌐▥⌐

The prosperous man is never sure that he is loved for himself. —
Latin Proverb.

—

The most pathetic people in the world are those who have everything to live with but nothing to live for.

—

Adversity makes men, and prosperity makes monsters. —Victor Hugo.

—

You can't take your money with you—but you can send it on ahead.

—

NO ONE IS SO POOR AS THE ONE WHO HAS NOTHING BUT MONEY.

—

Not what we have but what we enjoy constitutes our abundance.

—

The modern man drives a mortgaged car over a bond-financed highway on credit-card gasoline.

—

If you cannot have everything, make the best of everything you have.

—

Charity gives itself rich; covetousness hoards itself poor. —
German Proverb.

—

If your outgo exceeds your income, then your upkeep will be your downfall.

One man said, "My wife is kin to Teddy Roosevelt. She runs through the shopping center, yelling, 'Charge! Charge! Charge!'"

Some people are never satisfied with their lot in life until it is a lot more.

Millionaires who laugh are rare. My experience is that wealth is apt to take the smiles away. —Andrew Carnegie.

Show me a man who is looking for payday and sundown, and I'll show you a man who is not going to get very far in this world.

The only thing I have written that seems it will live forever is my signature on the home mortgage.

The most pathetic people in the world are those who have everything to live with but nothing to live for.

A Christian is one who does not have to consult his bank book to see how wealthy he really is.

Music

Speaking of modern-day music, a waiter dropped a tray full of dishes in a restaurant recently, and thirteen people got up and began to dance.

⌐▥┐

Even if rock 'n roll music died tomorrow, it would take five years for the sound to fade away.

⌐▥┐

Posted on a bulletin board at Penn Station: " FOR SALE—radio, record player and tape recorder. All in excellent condition. I'm the one who's broke."

⌐▥┐

Today it isn't facing the music that hurts, it's listening to it.

⌐▥┐

There is one thing to be said for this "modern music": you can't tell the difference when the record wears out.

⌐▥┐

So-called rock singers have the kind of voices that belong in silent films.

Old Age

When someone asked B. R. Lakin if he looked forward to

growing old, he replied, "Yes, especially when I consider the alternatives."

⌐𝗆𝗆⌐

A MAN IS YOUNG AT ANY AGE AS LONG AS HE CAN DREAM.

⌐𝗆𝗆⌐

Dr. Bob Jones, Sr., once said, "I don't feel old, but I can count."

⌐𝗆𝗆⌐

It's not how long you have been on the road but how far you've traveled.

⌐𝗆𝗆⌐

We cannot avoid growing OLD, but we can avoid growing COLD. —R. H. Stoll.

⌐𝗆𝗆⌐

Hardening of the heart ages people more quickly than hardening of the arteries.

⌐𝗆𝗆⌐

You are young only once, but you can remain immature indefinitely. —C.W.H.

⌐𝗆𝗆⌐

Regarding age I sometimes say, "I'm in the neighborhood of 30, but it's a big neighborhood." —C.W.H.

⌐𝗆𝗆⌐

You're an old-timer if you can remember when charity was a virtue and not an organization.

⌐𝗆𝗆⌐

TO STAY YOUTHFUL, STAY USEFUL.

⌐𝗆𝗆⌐

If you dread growing old, think of the many who never had that privilege.

Old age is when you get it all together and forget where you put it. —C.W.H.

Every dissipation of youth must be paid for with a draft on old age. —Bob Jones, Sr.

Middle age is when the broad mind and narrow waist exchange places.

One man said, "There are three sure signs of old age. First, you start forgetting things, and...uh...uh...I don't remember the other two."

Age is mind over matter; if you don't mind, it don't matter.

One man said, "It's terrible to grow old alone. My wife hasn't had a birthday in ten years."

HE WHO CONTROLS NOT HIS YOUTH WILL NOT ENJOY HIS OLD AGE.

You are reaching middle age when it takes longer to rest up than it did to get tired.

As soon as you become successful enough to sleep late, you are so old, you always wake up early.

‿𝄐‿

You are getting old when your back goes out more than you do.

‿𝄐‿

The biggest fault that older people find with the younger generation is that they no longer belong to it.

‿𝄐‿

A man once asked an attractive older lady, "And exactly what is your age?" She responded, "Can you keep a secret?" "Yes," he said; to which she replied, "So can I."

Opportunity

Somewhere I saw a sign that said, "Luck is preparation meeting opportunity."

‿𝄐‿

HOW EXCITING IT IS TO PASS THROUGH THE DOOR CHRIST OPENS!

‿𝄐‿

To the Israelites, Goliath is "too big to hit"; but to little David, he is "too big to miss."

‿𝄐‿

About the only thing that comes to him who waits is whiskers.

The trouble with an opportunity is that it is more recognizable going than it is coming.

You never get a second chance to make a good first impression.

Obstacles are what you see when you take your eyes off the goal.

Whatever your lot in life, why don't you try to build something on it?

Some people fail to recognize opportunity because it so often comes to them in overalls and looks like work.

Pastor, Preacher, Preaching

No sermon is dull that cuts the heart.

Every sermon should have a train of thought, but it should also have a terminal.

If you preach what is new, it won't be true. If you preach what is true, it won't be new. —Spurgeon.

When a preacher cannot get fire into his sermon, he should put the sermon into the fire.

Don't be squeamish in the pulpit—like one who said, "Jonah was three days and three nights in—ahem—the society of the fish." —Spurgeon.

I always like to act according to Cobbett's rule: "I speak not only so that I can be understood, but so that I cannot be misunderstood." —Spurgeon.

To be an effective preacher, be scriptural, be sincere, be simple, be short, and be seated. —C.W.H.

If you can smile while you skin them and make them smile while they are being skinned, they will follow you to the tannery to get the hide. —Sam Jones.

THE BEST INGREDIENT IN MOST SERMONS IS SHORTENING.

The preacher needs the head of a scholar, the heart of a child, and the hide of a rhinoceros.

A preacher who was in the habit of writing his sermons out carefully found himself at church one Sunday morning without his manuscript. "As I have forgotten my notes," he began his sermon, "I will have to rely on the Lord for guidance. Tonight I shall come better prepared."

PUT A GIRAFFE IN THE PULPIT AND THE LAMBS WILL STARVE TO DEATH.

There are some men who preach so well when in the pulpit, that it is a shame they should ever come out of it; and when they are out of it, they live so illy that it is a shame they should ever enter it. —Charles Wesley.

One man remarked to his pastor, "Every sermon you preach is better than the next one."

Someone suggested, "If you don't strike oil in thirty minutes, stop boring."

A Christian minister once said, "I was never of any use until I found out that God did not intend me to be a 'great man.'"

When liberty was offered to John Bunyan, then in prison, on condition of abstaining from preaching, he consistently replied, "If you let me out today, I shall preach again tomorrow."

The young unknown preacher, speaking for his first time in a big conference, said, "I feel like a 'Who's he?' in a group of 'Who's Who?'"

⌐▥⌐

Once in seven years I burn all my sermons; for it is a shame if I cannot write better sermons now than I did seven years ago. —John Wesley.

⌐▥⌐

There is a hatred which is downright charity; that is the hatred of erroneous doctrine. There is an intolerance which is downright praiseworthy; that is the intolerance of false doctrine in the pulpit. —Bishop J. C. Ryle.

⌐▥⌐

Someone reminded me that all my sermons have happy endings and then explained, "Everybody is happy when you finish." —C.W.H.

⌐▥⌐

Billy Sunday used to say, "Put the cookies on the lower shelf so everybody can reach them."

⌐▥⌐

One Sunday morning a lady said to the pastor, "I did not like your sermon this morning," to which he replied, "Neither did the Devil. Classify yourself and come back next Sunday."

⌐▥⌐

NO SERMON IS EVER QUITE A SUCCESS WHICH LEAVES MEN SATISFIED WITH THEMSELVES.

⌐▥⌐

The preacher's opening remark was, "I feel like the lightning bug who backed into the fan. I'm delighted to be here!"

⌐▥⌐

One preacher said, "I am bad to exaggerate. As a matter of fact, I have cried a bucket of tears over it!"

⌐ᴀᴀᴀ⌐

Dr. James Gray, when asked, "Where did you get that sermon?" replied, "I admit I milked twenty-one cows, but I made my own butter."

⌐ᴀᴀᴀ⌐

When a man shoots above the heads of the congregation, it doesn't prove he has superior ammunition; it only proves he has a bad aim.

⌐ᴀᴀᴀ⌐

Wesley, when once asked how he got the crowds, replied, "I set myself on fire, and people come to see me burn."

Patience

Patience is accepting a difficult situation without giving God a deadline to remove it. —Bill Gothard.

⌐ᴀᴀᴀ⌐

Patience is the ability to put up with what you want to put down.

⌐ᴀᴀᴀ⌐

The best thing about the future is that it comes only one day at a time. —Abraham Lincoln.

⌐ᴀᴀᴀ⌐

PATIENCE: the ability to idle your motor when you feel like stripping your gears.

___

Yard by yard is mighty hard, but inch by inch is a cinch.

Pessimist, Optimist

Blessed is the man who expects nothing, for he will never be disappointed. —Pope.

___

It seems that people always play up the bad side of things. Nobody ever puts up a sign that reads "NICE DOG."

___

The pessimist says, "If I don't try, I can't fail." The optimist says, "If I don't try, I can't win."

___

"I hear you have a good crop of potatoes this year, Mrs. Higgins. That must cheer your heart," said the neighbor. "Aye, they're good enough, but where's the bad'uns to feed the pigs?"

___

A pessimist is one who blows out the candle to see how dark it is.

___

I like the optimist who fell out the window of the 20th story floor and was heard to say as he passed the 2nd floor, "Safe so far!"

⸺

A pessimist is one who, when he smells flowers, looks around for a casket.

⸺

Definition of a pessimist: A man who has swallowed an egg; afraid to move for fear it will break; afraid to sit still for fear the thing will hatch.

⸺

The bald-headed optimist went into the drug store and asked for some hair restorer. When he started to leave, he said, "Oh, and by the way, I'll take two combs also."

⸺

A pessimist is someone whose daydreams are nightmares.

⸺

Both optimists and pessimists contribute to society. The optimist invents the airplane and the pessimist invents the parachute.

⸺

The spirit of optimism is the spirit that makes the tea kettle sing even when it is up to its neck in hot water!

⸺

The worst pest in the world is a pessimist. —C.W.H.

⸺

Somebody said, "An optimist is the fellow who takes the cold water thrown on his ideas, heats it with enthusiasm, makes steam and pushes ahead."

PESSIMISM: Looking at the world through woes-colored glasses.

One lady who complained about everything said, "I always feel bad even when I feel good because I know I'll feel bad again after while."

Prayer

A wise prayer: "Lord, fill my mouth with worthwhile stuff and nudge me when I've said enough. Amen."

When Jesus prayed in public, His prayers were always short. But when He prayed alone, His prayers were longer. On one occasion He continued all night to God in prayer. —C.W.H.

TAKE NO REST FROM PRAYER, AND GIVE HIM NO REST. —Spurgeon.

If you have so much business to attend to that you have no time to pray, you have more business on hand than God ever intended you should have. —Moody.

God may be out of sight, but He is certainly not out of reach: He is only a prayer away. —C.W.H.

Anchor yourself to the throne of God, then shorten the rope.

The best place to pray for potatoes is on the end of a hoe handle. —Bud Robinson.

One man, praying, said, "Lord, I haven't prayed in forty years; and if You'll answer my prayer this time, I won't bother You again for another forty years."

When we work, we get what we can do; but when we pray, we get what God can do.

"I was not looking at the little in hand, but at the fullness of God," said Mueller when his needs were great and the supply small.

PRAY FOR A POOR MEMORY WHEN PEOPLE SEEM UNKIND.

Every great movement of God can be traced to a kneeling figure. —D. L. Moody.

Prayer is the key to open the day and the bolt to shut in the night. —Bishop Taylor.

The possibilities of prayer exceed our ability to ask or even think (Eph. 3:20). —C.W.H.

⎯⎯

Groanings that cannot be uttered are often prayers which cannot be refused. —Spurgeon.

⎯⎯

True prayer should be a way of life, not just a case of emergency.

⎯⎯

I am sometimes startled at the power of a feeble prayer to win a speedy answer. —Spurgeon.

⎯⎯

Some folks are like the little boy who, when asked by his pastor if he prayed every day, replied, "No, not every day. Some days I don't want anything."

⎯⎯

Pray a definite prayer for a definite thing, meet definite conditions, exercise definite faith, and God will give a definite answer.

⎯⎯

Prayer is something more than asking God to run errands for us.

⎯⎯

If prayer will help me out of trouble, it will surely help me to keep out of trouble.

⎯⎯

When we pray for rain, we must be willing to put up with some mud.

⎯⎯

If I could hear Christ praying for me in the next room, I would not fear a million enemies; yet the distance makes no difference—He is praying for me. —McCheyne.

To pray about something and not make ourselves available is hypocrisy.

PRAYER IS NO SUBSTITUTE FOR DUTY.

Prayer is measured by depth, not length!

Nothing is discussed more and practiced less than prayer.

Salvation, Conversion

A Christian does good deeds, but just doing good deeds does not make a man a Christian. —Bob Jones, Sr.

God is in the cleansing business, not the whitewashing business.

Absolute dependence on what God has done equals salvation; absolute dependence on what God has said equals assurance. —C.W.H.

The religions of the world say, "do and live." The religion of the Bible says, "live and do." —Bob Jones, Sr.

⎯▥⎯

Religion is the best armor a man can have, but it is the worst cloak. —John Bunyan.

⎯▥⎯

Although God created man without man's help, He will not save man without man's consent.

⎯▥⎯

We don't go to Heaven head first but heart first. — Tom Malone, Sr.

⎯▥⎯

It is just as easy to climb to Heaven from a molehill as it is from the top of Mount Everest. You can do neither. —C.W.H.

⎯▥⎯

You don't spell *salvation* "D-O." You spell it "D-O-N-E." —C.W.H.

⎯▥⎯

Deathbed repentance is burning the candle of life in the service of the Devil, then blowing the smoke into the face of God. — Billy Sunday.

⎯▥⎯

BETTER NEVER TO HAVE BEEN BORN AT ALL, THAN NEVER TO HAVE BEEN BORN AGAIN.

⎯▥⎯

Most anybody can put a new suit of clothes on a man, but only God can put a new man in a suit of clothes.

⎯▥⎯

Justification is something that cannot be reversed and followed by damnation.

If we put off repentance another day, we have a day more to repent of, and a day less to repent in. —Mason.

Trying to earn salvation by our goodness is like putting a drop of perfume in an ocean of filth. —C.W.H.

I don't know I'm saved because I feel good; I know I'm saved because the Bible says so; and I feel good because I know I'm saved. —Bob Jones, Sr.

Salvation may come in quietly, but few people can keep quiet about it. —C.W.H.

The salvation that Jesus Christ purchased for a lost world is wonderful in its magnitude. It is as deep as fallen humanity, as broad as the compassion of God, as high as Heaven, and as everlasting as the eternal Rock of Ages. —Uncle Bud Robinson.

You have not been high-born until you have been born from on High. —Bob Jones, Sr.

MANY WHO EXPECT TO BE SAVED IN THE ELEVENTH HOUR DIE AT TEN-THIRTY.

Christ knocks at my door here, and I knock at His door over there. If I open to Him here, He will open to me over there. Isn't that fair? —Uncle Bud Robinson.

Self

Under the Constitution of the United States every man has the right to make a fool of himself as he sees fit.

Many people believe that admitting a fault means they no longer have to correct it.

Don't go around with a chip on your shoulder—people might think it came off your head.

When we expect more of others than we expect of ourselves, we are in a state of carnality.

What you are is not nearly as important as *whose* you are.

Self always wants to be crowned, but God says it must be crucified.

He who forgets his friend is ungrateful to him, but he who forgets his Saviour is unmerciful to himself. —Bunyan.

CONFESSING YOUR SINS IS NO SUBSTITUTE FOR FORSAKING THEM.

Charles Simmons gave us a sentence sermon when he wrote, "No man has a right to do as he pleases, except when he pleases to do right."

When a man won't listen to his conscience, it's usually because he doesn't want advice from a total stranger.

The Greeks said, "Know thyself." The Romans said, "Control thyself." Christ said, "Deny thyself."

Who has deceived thee so oft as thyself? —Benjamin Franklin.

If a hypocrite is between you and Heaven, then he's closer to Heaven than you are.

Big shots are small shots who keep on shooting.

MANY PEOPLE ARE SUFFERING FROM SELF-INFLICTED WOUNDS.

I have never met a man who has given me as much trouble as myself. —D. L. Moody.

Everyone thinks of changing the world, but no one thinks of changing himself. —Leo Tolstoy.

I always like to hear a man talk about himself, because then I never hear anything but good. —Will Rogers.

One man complained, "I am the kind of person who, if it were raining soup, I would be standing there with a fork."

He who falls in love with himself is not apt to have much competition.

It is all right to talk with yourself, but you are in trouble when you start asking questions.

I like to talk to myself for two reasons. First, I like to hear intelligent people talk; and second, I like to talk to intelligent people. —John R. Rice.

Some people think they are big shots just because they explode with a loud noise!

No man who thinks in terms of catching mice will ever catch lions.

GIVE SOME PEOPLE AN INCH, AND THEY THINK THEY ARE RULERS.

.ᴄᴍ.

We are all dangerous folk without God's controlling hand. —
William Ward Ayer.

Service

The will of God will never lead us where the grace of God is inadequate to keep us.

.ᴄᴍ.

"You can never do more than your duty," said Robert E. Lee, "and you should never wish to do less."

.ᴄᴍ.

SERVICE CAN NEVER BECOME SLAVERY TO ONE WHO LOVES. —J. L. Massee.

.ᴄᴍ.

If God has called you, do not spend time looking over your shoulder to see who is following.

.ᴄᴍ.

It is more important to be than to do. You can do without being but you can't be without doing. —C.W.H.

.ᴄᴍ.

SERVE FOR THE GOOD YOU CAN DO, NOT FOR THE PRAISE
YOU GET.

⌐ɱɱ⌐

The higher you rise in the likeness of Jesus, the lower you will
stoop in your service for others.

⌐ɱɱ⌐

Do what you can, where you are, with what you have.

⌐ɱɱ⌐

The woods would be very silent if no birds sang there except
those that sang best.

⌐ɱɱ⌐

Slight not what's near while aiming at what's far.

⌐ɱɱ⌐

The most important light in the house is not the chandelier in
the parlor. It's that little back hall light that keeps you from
breaking your neck when you go to the bathroom in the middle of the night. —Bob Jones, Sr.

⌐ɱɱ⌐

THE BEST ABILITY IS AVAILABILITY. —C.W.H.

⌐ɱɱ⌐

Have your tools ready; God will find you work. —*Gospel Message.*

⌐ɱɱ⌐

*Reward for Christian service is based on faithfulness to oppor-
tunity given.* —C.W.H.

⌐ɱɱ⌐

He who serves God for money will serve the Devil for higher wages.

The sun, with all those planets revolving around it and dependent upon it, can still ripen a bunch of grapes as if it had nothing else in the universe to do. —Galileo.

The measure of your responsibilities is a measure of your opportunities. —Bob Jones, Sr.

The real tragedy of life is not in being limited to one talent, but in the failure to use the one talent.

WHAT A BIG DIFFERENCE THERE IS BETWEEN GIVING ADVICE AND LENDING A HAND!

A good rule to follow: give God the first part of every day, the first day of every week, and the first part of your income. —C.W.H.

God never puts any man in a place too small to grow in.

Our Lord was a willing Saviour, and He uses only willing servants. —C.W.H.

GOD DOESN'T CALL THE FIT; HE FITS THE CALLED.

When the good takes the place of the best, even the good becomes
bad.

*We need the eagerness to serve like that of a hunting dog awaiting
a chase.*

Sin, Worldliness, Temptation

*Temptation is not a sin. It only becomes a sin when it is yielded
to. Even our Lord was tempted.* —C.W.H.

Stay away from the precipice! You can't alter the inevitable! If
you lean too far out of the window, they'll call the coroner!
If you eat salt herring, even the grace of God won't keep you
from being thirsty! Eat raw onions, and even the grace of
God won't give you the sweet breath of a baby! Some things
are INEVITABLE!

*You can find the world's shortest sermon on a thousand traffic
signs: KEEP RIGHT.* —Amarillo News.

When a man has not a good reason for doing a thing, he has
one good reason for letting it alone. —Sir Walter Scott.

God will lower the gate of warning, sound the bell, flash the red light, but He won't keep you from crossing the tracks.

⌐▥⌐

WE GAIN THE STRENGTH OF THE TEMPTATION WE RESIST.

⌐▥⌐

Sin is a heart disease that can only be permanently remedied by the Great Physician.

⌐▥⌐

The lust of the flesh is a consuming desire *to do.* The lust of the eyes is a compelling urge *to have.* The pride of life is a constant thrust *to be.*

⌐▥⌐

When in doubt play safe. —Bob Jones, Sr.

⌐▥⌐

Christ died for sin; the believer dies to sin; the unbeliever dies in sin. —D. L. Moody.

⌐▥⌐

The disease of an evil conscience is beyond the practice of all the physicians of all the countries in the world. —W. E. Gladstone.

⌐▥⌐

A ship is safe in the ocean as long as the ocean is not in the ship. And a Christian is safe in the world so long as the world is not in the Christian.

⌐▥⌐

It wasn't the apple on the tree that caused all the trouble; it was the pair on the ground.

⌐▥⌐

By yielding to temptation, one may lose in a moment what it took him a lifetime to gain.

A prisoner mending his trousers was asked, "Are you sewing?" "No," he replied, "I'm reaping."

Whosoever sows to the flesh must pluck the thistles of his own sowing. He will be thrashed, scratched and bruised by the thorns of his own misdeeds.

SIN IN A CHRISTIAN'S LIFE MAKES A COWARD OF HIM.

Christ cannot reign in the parlor of our hearts while we entertain the Devil in the cellar of our thoughts.

One of the worst things about sin for the Christian is that it weakens our moral and spiritual resistance. —C.W.H.

Sin: a moment of gratification; an eternity of remorse.

Someone said, "The reason a certain person is so short is because the Bible says, 'The wicked shall be cut off.'"

It is easier to suppress the first desire than to satisfy all that follow it. —Franklin.

WILD OATS NEED NO FERTILIZER.

A gash in the conscience may disfigure a soul forever. —Spurgeon.

Bad things in life are enjoyed first and paid for later, but good things in life are paid for first, then later enjoyed.

Right is right, even if everyone is against it; and wrong is wrong, even if everyone is for it.

No one can honestly or hopefully be delivered from temptation unless he has himself honestly and firmly determined to do the best he can to keep out of it. —Ruskin.

You cannot think dirty, you cannot talk dirty, you cannot act dirty—and be clean!

Temptations, when first we meet them, are as a lion that roared upon Samson, but if we overcome them, the next time we see them, we shall find a nest of honey within. —John Bunyan.

THE TIME IS NEVER RIGHT TO DO A WRONG THING.

One thing to be sure of—there will be no reduction in the wages of sin.

To explain why you backslid does not justify it.

Some people have yet to learn that they cannot travel in the wrong direction and reach the right destination.

⌐ₐₘ₋

The Devil always gets out a few extra copies when a saint goes wrong.

⌐ₐₘ₋

If we cover our sin, God will uncover it; if we uncover it to God, He will cover it with His blood.

⌐ₐₘ₋

It is a sin to do less than your best. —Bob Jones, Sr.

⌐ₐₘ₋

Better shun the bait than struggle in the snare. —Dryden.

⌐ₐₘ₋

The further a man goes in lust and iniquity, the more dead he becomes to purity and holiness. He loses the power to appreciate the beauties of virtue or to be disgusted with abominations of vice. —Spurgeon.

⌐ₐₘ₋

Where modesty is absent, virtue has no means of protection.

⌐ₐₘ₋

Sin must be dealt with in one of two ways—punishment or pardon.

⌐ₐₘ₋

DO NOT BLAME GOD FOR THE HARVEST WHEN YOU DO THE SOWING.

⌐ₐₘ₋

The greatest security against sin is to be shocked at its presence. —Carlyle.

‿ᴏᴏ‿

Love can wait to give, but lust can't wait to get.

Success, Failure

The door to the room of success swings on the hinges of opposition. —Bob Jones, Sr.

‿ᴏᴏ‿

Look forward to some success, not backward at any failure.

‿ᴏᴏ‿

The emergency against which I shall most carefully provide is failure. —David Livingstone.

‿ᴏᴏ‿

The greatest lessons are learned from our failures; we very seldom learn anything from our successes.

‿ᴏᴏ‿

Out of the will of God there is no such thing as success; in the will of God there cannot be any failures.

‿ᴏᴏ‿

The average man has five senses: touch, taste, sight, smell and hearing. The successful man has two more: horse and common.

⌐ᴨᴨ⌐

Never make a plan without seeking God's guidance; never achieve a success without giving Him the praise.

⌐ᴨᴨ⌐

Someone said success is relative—the more success the more relatives!

⌐ᴨᴨ⌐

Success comes in *cans.* That's right, because failure comes in *can'ts.*

⌐ᴨᴨ⌐

THE ONLY TIME SUCCESS COMES BEFORE WORK IS IN THE DICTIONARY.

⌐ᴨᴨ⌐

The man who fails and still fights on is able to turn temporary defeats into permanent success.

⌐ᴨᴨ⌐

When you have made your mark in the world, watch out for guys with erasers. —*Wall Street Journal.*

⌐ᴨᴨ⌐

I learned one thing at the post office: the postage stamp is a success because it sticks to one thing. —C.W.H.

⌐ᴨᴨ⌐

Napoleon succeeded because there was a little Napoleon in every Frenchman. —Spurgeon.

⌐ᴨᴨ⌐

Success is finding God's will and doing it. —Bob Jones, Sr.

A mistake is evidence that someone has tried to do something.

No man can soar higher than he is able to think by the grace of God. —Bob Jones, Sr.

PROMOTION IS TWO-THIRDS "MOTION."

I don't like these cold, precise, perfect people who, in order not to speak wrong, never speak at all; and in order not to do wrong, never do anything. —Beecher.

Make chariot wheels out of your failures and ride them to success.

Success is measured by what we are as compared to what we could be. —C.W.H.

Success is to be measured not so much by the position that one has reached in life as by the obstacles which he has overcome while trying to succeed. —Booker T. Washington.

The men who try to do something and fail, are infinitely better than those who try to do nothing and succeed. —Lloyd Jones.

Learn from the mistakes of others—you won't live long enough to make them all yourself.

Repeated victories over your problems are rungs on the ladder of success. —C.W.H.

Happy is the man whose ambitions do not exceed his abilities.

Failure is the one thing that can be achieved without much effort.

Everybody makes mistakes; that is the reason they put erasers on pencils.

FAILURE IS SUCCESS WITH A FRESH COAT OF PAINT ON IT.

A definite purpose is the beginning point of all success. —C.W.H.

No man ever progresses beyond the point where he is willing to admit failure. —C.W.H.

The road to success is dotted with many tempting parking places.

No one is a failure who can truly say, "I have done my best."

Those who complain about the way the ball bounces are often the ones who dropped it.

Sunday School

The Sunday school teacher said, "Lot's wife looked back and turned into a pillar of salt." One of her young students said, "That's nothing! My mother looked back and turned into a telephone pole."

One little boy, when asked, "Who was sorry when the prodigal son returned home?" replied, "The fatted calf."

A little boy in my Sunday school quoted Matthew 11:28, "Come unto me, all ye that labor and are heavy laden, and I will do the rest." —C.W.H.

One little boy, when asked if he would rather be the rich man or Lazarus, replied, "I'd like to be the rich man while I'm alive and Lazarus when I'm dead."

Temper, Anger, Wrath, Hatred

Good men are reasonable men. When a man ceases to be reasonable, he is no longer good. —Bob Jones, Sr.

JEALOUSY DIGS THE MUD THAT ENVY THROWS AT SUCCESS. —C.W.H.

One of the marks of a gentleman is his refusal to make an issue out of every difference of opinion. —Arnold H. Glascow.

I will not permit any man to narrow and degrade my soul by making me hate him. —Booker T. Washington.

Those who differ with me have caused me to learn more than those who have agreed with me in everything.

No one has been able to stand up indefinitely under the weight of carrying a grudge.

For every minute you are angry you lose sixty seconds of happiness.

Our temper is one of the few things that improves the longer we keep it. —W. B. Knight.

You cannot couple abiding wrath with annihilation. —C.W.H.

Anger is more active than gratitude. People are not hesitant to express their anger but very seldom express their gratitude. —C.W.H.

ENVY SHOOTS AT OTHERS AND WOUNDS ITSELF.

People who fly into a rage always make a bad landing. —Will Rogers.

Hatred does a great deal more damage to the vessel in which it is stored than the object on which it is poured.

Jealousy is the child of love but envy is the child of hate. —C.W.H.

Meekness is giving a soft answer to a rough question. —W. B. Knight.

Temper is that which brings out the best in steel and the worst in man.

Speak when you are angry and you will make the best speech you will ever regret.

A TEMPER DISPLAYED IN PUBLIC IS INDECENT EXPOSURE.

An angry man is seldom reasonable; a reasonable man is seldom angry.

Someone said, "I'm temperamental." That's 90% temper and 10% mental.

To ignore an insult is a good test of moral courage.

⌐᠊ᠬᠬ᠊⌐

People green with envy are ripe for trouble.

Thanks, Gratitude

It has been well said that we write our benefits in dust and our injuries in marble.

⌐᠊ᠬᠬ᠊⌐

All that is required to make some unmindful of God's blessings is to receive them so often and so regularly.

⌐᠊ᠬᠬ᠊⌐

TO THE DISCONTENTED MAN, NO CHAIR IS EASY. —Benjamin Franklin.

⌐᠊ᠬᠬ᠊⌐

A gentleman, traveling on a misty morning, asked a shepherd what weather it will be. "It will be," said the shepherd, "what weather pleaseth me." Asked to explain, the shepherd said, "Sir, it shall be what weather pleases God; and what weather pleases God also pleases me." —Foster.

⌐᠊ᠬᠬ᠊⌐

A bad moment for an atheist is when he feels grateful and has no one to thank.

⌐᠊ᠬᠬ᠊⌐

Contentment is a good thing—until it sits in the shade and lets the weeds grow. When it reaches that point, it has gone too far!

⌐ᴨᴨ˥

He who is not grateful for the good things he has, would not be happy with what he wishes he had.

⌐ᴨᴨ˥

Gratitude is the loveliest flower in the garden of man's soul; and when gratitude dies on the altar of a man's heart, he is well nigh gone. —Bob Jones, Sr.

⌐ᴨᴨ˥

If you want to feel rich, just count all the things you have that money can't buy. —Daniel Webster.

⌐ᴨᴨ˥

If a man could make a single rose, we would give him an empire; yet flowers no less beautiful are scattered in profusion over the world and no one regards them. —Martin Luther.

⌐ᴨᴨ˥

I grumbled because I had to get up in the morning—until one morning I couldn't get up.

⌐ᴨᴨ˥

When you have nothing left but God, then for the first time you become aware that God is enough.

⌐ᴨᴨ˥

It isn't what you have in your pocket that makes you thankful; it's what you have in your heart.

Time

Time to me is so precious that with great difficulty can I steal one hour in eight days either to satisfy myself or to gratify my friends. —John Knox.

How you spend your time is more important than how you spend your money. Financial mistakes can be corrected, but time is gone forever.

Years ago if people missed a stagecoach they were content to wait two or three days for the next one. Now they have a nervous breakdown if they miss one section in a revolving door.

THE ROAD TO BY-AND-BY LEADS TO THE HOUSE OF NEVER.

We always find time to do the things we really believe are important. —C.W.H.

What you put off today, you'll probably also put off tomorrow.

A man who is too busy for God is just too busy!

If you don't have time to do it right, how will you find time to
   do it over? —C.W.H.

⌐ɷ⌐

The Lord wants our precious time, not our spare time.

⌐ɷ⌐

LOST TIME IS NEVER FOUND.

⌐ɷ⌐

Yesterday is a canceled check, tomorrow is a promissory note,
   today is the only cash we have, so spend it wisely.

⌐ɷ⌐

Another year is but another call from God.

⌐ɷ⌐

The difference between yesterday and tomorrow is today.

⌐ɷ⌐

*Turn backward, turn backward, O time in thy run, for now I can
   see how it should have been done!* —Elinor K. Rose.

⌐ɷ⌐

Americans have more time-saving devices and less time than
   any other people in the world.

⌐ɷ⌐

Procrastination is a thief of time.

Tongue

Nothing is easier than fault-finding: no talent, no self-denial, no brains, no character are required to set up in the grumbling business.

Raised voices lower esteem. Hot tempers cool friendships. Loose tongues stretch truth. Swelled heads shrink influence. Sharp words dull respect.

Never judge a man by what he says; try to find out why he said it.

The most valuable of all talents is that of never using two words when one will do. —Thomas Jefferson.

If your foot slips, you may recover your balance, but if your tongue slips, you cannot recall your words.

There is the story of a lady who never spoke ill of anybody. "I believe you would say something good even about the Devil," a friend told her. "Well," she said, "you certainly do have to admire his persistence."

The man who parrots another's opinions instead of arriving at his own is not wise—he's just likewise.

The tongue can bring more calm than tranquilizing pills. On the other hand, it can bring more destruction than the nuclear bomb. —Richard L. Rothman.

A LOOSE TONGUE OFTEN GETS IN A TIGHT PLACE.

It is better to say a good thing about a bad fellow, than to say a bad thing about a good fellow.

You can't tell by the honk of the horn how much gas is in the tank. —C.W.H.

A blow with a word strikes deeper than a blow with a sword. — Robert Burton.

Someone suggested that tact is the ability not to say what you really think.

A MAN WHO SAYS WHAT HE THINKS MAY BE COURAGEOUS BUT FRIENDLESS.

Tact is the ability to idle your engine when you really want to strip a gear.

We are not only responsible for what we say but for what people understand us to say.

Talk is cheap if it is not lawyers who are doing the talking.

Tact is the ability to shut your mouth before somebody wants to shut it for you.

One minute of keeping your mouth shut is worth one hour of explanation!

The more you say, the less people remember. The fewer the words, the greater the profit. —Fenelon.

About the only exercise some people get is side-stepping respon-sibility, running down their neighbors, and jumping to conclusions.

Some talkative people never discover why they were given two ears and only one tongue.

If I stop to think before I speak, I won't have to worry afterward about what I said.

IT OFTEN SHOWS A FINE COMMAND OF LANGUAGE TO SAY NOTHING.

> Be careful of the words you say,
> To keep them soft and sweet;
> You never know from day to day
> Which ones you'll have to eat!

Some people would say more if they talked less.

⌐∩∩⌐

Learning to speak in several different languages is not nearly as valuable as learning to keep your mouth shut in one.

⌐∩∩⌐

One man complained, "My wife's mouth is so big it takes her 45 minutes to put on lipstick."

⌐∩∩⌐

PEOPLE WITH SHARP TONGUES OFTEN END UP CUTTING THEIR OWN THROATS.

⌐∩∩⌐

Many who boast about having an open mind often have an open mouth to match.

Trials, Tribulations

A man's real courage shows to best advantage in his hour of adversity. —C.W.H.

⌐∩∩⌐

Christian persecution is not trouble in general. Everybody has that. Christian persecution is trouble that you get into that you would not have gotten into if you hadn't been a Christian. —Vance Havner.

⌐∩∩⌐

How you handle your problems by day determines how you sleep by night.

⌐ℿ¬

Do not ask God to give you a lighter burden; ask Him to give you strong shoulders to carry a heavier burden. —Bob Jones, Sr.

⌐ℿ¬

Putting the tea bag in hot water doesn't cause it to turn dark; it only brings out the darkness that was already there. —C.W.H.

⌐ℿ¬

As long as I keep my face toward the light, the shadows will fall behind me. —John M. Younginer.

⌐ℿ¬

The world is not interested in the storms you encountered, but did you bring in the ship?

⌐ℿ¬

It is not so much the greatness of our troubles as the littleness of our spirit which makes us complain. —J. Taylor.

⌐ℿ¬

The gem cannot be polished without friction, nor the child of God perfected without adversity.

⌐ℿ¬

Squeezing the lemon does not make it sour; it only brings out what was already there. —C.W.H.

⌐ℿ¬

No physician ever weighed out medicine to his patients with half so much care and exactness as God weighs out to us every trial. Not one grain too much does He ever permit to be put in the scale. —Henry Ward Beecher.

Often our trials act as a thorn hedge to keep us in the good pasture; but our prosperity is a gap through which we go astray. —C. H. Spurgeon.

The Devil promises glory without suffering, but God promises glory through suffering. —C.W.H.

TRIALS DO NOT NECESSARILY MAKE US; THEY ONLY RE-VEAL US.

Problems point out failures and weaknesses.

The next time trouble seems to overwhelm you, remember the tea kettle. Although up to its neck in hot water, it continues to whistle.

When there's trouble, some folks meet it; others pull up stakes and beat it.

Jesus Christ is no security against storms, but He is a perfect security in storms.

Some people are happy to suffer in silence if they are sure everyone knows they are doing it.

The presence of a brave man in the time of trouble is a comfort to his companions.

Much of the trouble of this life can be traced to saying "yes" too quick and not saying "no" soon enough.

You can save yourself a lot of trouble by not borrowing any.

No matter how stony the path, some forge ahead; no matter how easy the way, some lag behind.

God uses the gymnasium of trouble to equip us for the race of life. —C.W.H.

GREAT TRIALS ARE OFTEN NECESSARY TO PREPARE US FOR GREAT RESPONSIBILITIES.

God never promised us a journey without storms; He only promised a safe crossing. —C.W.H.

"What is life's heaviest burden?" asked a youth to a sad and lonely old man. His answer: "To have nothing to carry."

Problems are opportunities for improvement. —C.W.H.

Blessed is the man who knows how to make stepping stones out of stumbling stones. —Bob Jones, Sr.

Truth

There must come, with decision for truth, a corresponding protest against error. —Spurgeon.

Anything short of truth and anything beyond the truth is a lie. —C.W.H.

We may have three principal objects in the study of truth: (1) to discover it when we seek it; (2) to demonstrate it when we have found it; and (3) to distinguish it from error when we examine it. —Blaise Pascal.

Some people can take a slap in the face a lot better than they can take a pat on the back. —C.W.H.

TRUTH DOES NOT NEED DEFENSE—IT ONLY NEEDS WITNESSES.

The man who sincerely and unselfishly desires to know what's right doesn't have any trouble finding out what's right. — Bob Jones, Sr.

Prejudice is a great time-saver. It enables you to form opinions without bothering to get the facts.

⌐ᴰᴰᴰ⌐

NOTHING RUINS THE TRUTH LIKE STRETCHING IT.

⌐ᴰᴰᴰ⌐

Truth's most becoming garment is simplicity. —Bob Jones, Sr.

Witnessing, Evangelism, Revival

Every Christian is a missionary—if only to the supermarket.

⌐ᴰᴰᴰ⌐

Gamaliel Bradford said of D. L. Moody: "He looked in the face of more men than any man who ever lived and reduced Hell's prospective population by a million souls."

⌐ᴰᴰᴰ⌐

Revival is the result of the proper use of constituted means. —C.W.H.

⌐ᴰᴰᴰ⌐

When the power of prayer, the power of the Word of God, and the power of the Holy Spirit are at work, revival is at hand.

⌐ᴰᴰᴰ⌐

It is the Christian's business to populate Heaven and to depopulate Hell. —C.W.H.

⌐ᴰᴰᴰ⌐

It is almost the easiest thing in the world to lead a child from five to ten years of age to a definite acceptance of Christ. — R. A. Torrey.

IT TAKES EVANGELISTIC UNCTION TO MAKE ORTHODOXY FUNCTION. —Bob Jones, Sr.

Justification is only the removal of an obstacle in the believer's life so that God can fulfill His purpose through us, which is fruit-bearing—winning others to Christ. —C.W.H.

That land is henceforth my country which most needs the Gospel. —Count Zinzendorf.

The only generation that can reach this generation is our generation. —Oswald J. Smith.

The wisest man's description of a wise man is found in Proverbs 11:30: "He that winneth souls is wise." —C.W.H.

If called to be a missionary, don't stoop to be a king. —Spurgeon.

A soul winner is one who never gets used to the sound of marching feet on the way to a lost eternity.

Christ's last act before death was winning a soul, His last command was to win souls, and His last prayer was forgiveness for a soul.

Some want to live within the sound of church or chapel bell; I want to run a rescue shop within a yard of Hell. —C. T. Studd.

On the flyleaf of one famous pastor's Bible are these words: "They will not seek, they must be sought; they will not come, they must be brought; they will not study, they must be taught."

Look on visitation as a business, not an incidental matter; as work, not play; as time well spent, not wasted; as a privilege, not a boresome duty. —R. G. Lee.

We can never evangelize the world until the evangelized become evangelists. —C.W.H.

It is impossible to send the Gospel to the wrong place. —Wm. Troup.

The monument I want after I am dead is one with two legs going around the world—a saved sinner telling about the salvation of Jesus Christ. —D. L. Moody.

They tried to stamp out the fire of God in Jerusalem, but they scattered the embers all over the world. —Harold L. Lundquist.

THE ONLY ALTERNATIVE TO SOUL WINNING IS DISOBE-DIENCE TO CHRIST. —C.W.H.

We visit a lot of people we never get, but we get a lot of people we never visit; but we would never get a lot of people we never visit if we didn't visit a lot of people we never get. —C.W.H.

Where there is one who does not know Jesus Christ, there is a mission field.

The bringing of one soul to Jesus is the highest achievement possible to human life. —George W. Truett.

Soul winning is a personal responsibility. You can no more win souls by proxy than you can be baptized or tithe by proxy. —C.W.H.

CHRIST INVITES YOU TO COME BUT COMMANDS YOU TO GO.

This generation of saints is going to answer to God for this generation of sinners. —C.W.H.

If your Christianity is worth having, it should be worth sharing.

Work

Jesus never taught men how to make a living; He taught men how to live. —Bob Jones, Sr.

Everybody wants to start at the top. But the only two jobs I know where you start at the top are well-digging and grave-digging. —C.W.H.

⸺

Blessed is the man who keeps looking for work after he has found a job!

⸺

Some people are so lazy that, if their ship did come in, they would be too lazy to unload it.

⸺

Thinking is the hardest work there is, which is the probable reason so few engage in it. —Henry Ford.

⸺

The height of laziness is a fellow who gets up at five in the morning so he can have more time to loaf.

⸺

God calls men when they are busy, and Satan calls them when they are idle.

⸺

A famous athlete once said, "There's no way to make up for lost practice."

⸺

A man is not paid for having hands and head, but for using them.

⸺

There seems to be an ambition on the part of many to learn "the tricks of the trade" rather than the trade.

⸺

Dreaming has its values, but never should it become a substitute for work that needs to be done.

⌐ᴁᴁ⌐

Maybe we wouldn't need a machine that does the work of fifty people if fifty people did the work of fifty people!

⌐ᴁᴁ⌐

If you want your dreams to come true, don't oversleep.

⌐ᴁᴁ⌐

HE WHO WORKS THE OARS SELDOM ROCKS THE BOAT.

⌐ᴁᴁ⌐

Someone said, "Work doesn't bother me. I can lie down next to it and go to sleep."

⌐ᴁᴁ⌐

One man said, "I am working for a good cause—'cause I need the money."

⌐ᴁᴁ⌐

Nobody ever became "Man of the Hour" by watching the clock.

⌐ᴁᴁ⌐

How busy is not so important as *why* busy. The bee is praised; the mosquito is swatted.

⌐ᴁᴁ⌐

Sign at the entrance of a great manufacturing plant reads:

IF YOU ARE LIKE A WHEELBARROW—GOING NO
FARTHER THAN YOU ARE PUSHED—YOU
NEED NOT APPLY FOR WORK HERE

⌐ᴁᴁ⌐

After all is said and done, more is said than done.

⌐ɱɱ⌐

If you want to kill time, why not try working it to death? —
E. C. McKenzie.

⌐ɱɱ⌐

*A good thing to remember, a better thing to do—work with the
construction gang, not with the wrecking crew.*

⌐ɱɱ⌐

The best kind of pride is that which compels a man to do his
best work even though no one is looking.

⌐ɱɱ⌐

*Somewhere I read that on the face of Sir Walter Scott's watch
was written, "Work for the night is coming when no man can
work."*

⌐ɱɱ⌐

LIFE, LIKE A MIRROR, NEVER GIVES BACK MORE THAN WE
PUT INTO IT.

⌐ɱɱ⌐

*He who would leave footprints on the sands of time must wear
work shoes.*

⌐ɱɱ⌐

There are so many labor-saving devices on the market today that
a man has to work all his life to pay for them.

⌐ɱɱ⌐

*No man is born into the world whose work is not born with
him.* —James Russell Lowell.

⌐ɱɱ⌐

Nothing will ever be attempted if all possible objections must be first overcome. —Samuel Johnson.

Someone gave this definition of a boss: One who is late when you are early and early when you are late.

Tomorrow would promise to be the busiest day of the year. — Spanish Proverb.

God will not do for you what He has given you strength to do for yourself. —Bob Jones, Sr.

A diamond is a piece of coal that stuck to the job.

Even if you are on the right track, you will get run over if you just sit there.

FINISH THE JOB. —Bob Jones, Sr.

A bushelful of resolutions is of small value; a single grain of practice is worth the whole. —Spurgeon.

The Christian's works will be tried for *sort,* not for *size.* God is more interested in quality than He is in quantity. —C.W.H.

The wagon that makes the loudest noise has the lightest load.

A man may have too much money or too much honor, but he cannot have too much grace. —Spurgeon.

A man can do more work than he thinks he can, but he usually does less than he thinks he does.

The world expects results. Don't tell them about the labor pains—show them the baby. —Arnold Glascow.

I rise early because no day is long enough for a day's work. — Justice Bfandeis.

He who rises late must trot all day. —Benjamin Franklin.

When I was a young man, I observed that nine out of ten things I did were failures. Not wanting to be a failure, I did ten times more work. —George Bernard Shaw.

There has never yet been a man in our history who led a life of ease whose name is worth remembering. —Theodore Roosevelt.

If you worked for your employer as you serve God, how long would you hold your job?

Welfare rolls are made from our dough. —Paul Harvey.

God will not contribute to our delinquency by supplying us with gifts which we could get for ourselves but have done nothing to obtain.

His biographer said of Sir Walter Scott, "He could toil terribly."

One bad thing about doing nothing is that you can never take a day off.

FEW PEOPLE MAKE FOOTPRINTS ON THE SANDS OF TIME WEARING LOAFERS.

A fellow pulling on the oars hasn't time to rock the boat. —C.W.H.

It isn't the number of hours that a man puts in but what a man puts in the hours that counts.

God gives every bird food, but He does not throw it into the nest. —J. G. Holland.

The man who wakes up and finds himself famous hasn't been asleep.

Worry

When you worry you are just paying interest on nothing.

Today is the tomorrow you worried about yesterday.

One man decided to put a marble in a vase for each worry during the year. At the end of the year he had quite a collection of marbles, but he couldn't remember what worry even one of them represented. —R. T. Green.

WHEN YOU GET WRINKLED WITH CARE AND WORRY, IT'S TIME TO HAVE A FAITH LIFT.

We would worry less about what others think of us if we realized how seldom they do.

Worry never accomplishes anything except wrinkles—which gives you something else to worry about.

Worry is like a rocking chair: it gives you something to do but doesn't get you anywhere.

When a middle-age man says he's worried about the fallout, he probably means hair, not atoms.

WORRY IS USING TODAY'S STRENGTH ON TOMORROW'S PROBLEMS. —C.W.H.

Schedule all your worrying for a specific half hour about the middle of the day, then take a nap during that period.

You cannot change the past, but you can ruin a perfectly good present by worrying about it.

How wonderful life would be if we could forget our troubles as easily as we forget our blessings.

Miscellaneous

Our generation has seen television go from infancy to adultery.

The neurotic builds castles in the sky; the psychotic lives in them; the psychiatrist collects the rent.

Sign in office of one of our largest downtown buildings: *Remember the Energy Crisis. Please turn off lights when not in use. Thanks a Watt.*

The trouble with being a good sport is that you have to lose to prove it.

A lawyer is a man who will read a 10,000-word document and call it "a brief."

The nearest way to a man's heart is through his stomach.

The most likely way to obtain perfection is to follow the advice we give to others.

Dodging the future in this world is a success equal to that of the old woman who triumphantly declared that she had borrowed enough money to pay all her debts.

The chances are about 10 to 1 that when a man slaps you on the back, he wants you to cough up something.

ONE MAY GO WRONG IN MANY DIRECTIONS BUT RIGHT IN ONLY ONE.

Open-minded or empty-headed; it depends on whether you're defining yourself or someone else.

If not a single cock crows, will daylight fail to appear? —Malay Proverb.

One man said, "All I know about the speed of light is that it gets here too early in the morning."

Sign on the window of a men's clothing store that went bankrupt after three months in business: OPENED BY MISTAKE.

Get thy brother's boat across and, lo, thine own boat hath reached the shore.

The human race has been able to improve everything but people.

They are never alone who are accompanied by noble thoughts. —Sydney.

A celebrity is a person who works hard all his life to become well known, then wears dark glasses to avoid being recognized.

Car sickness is sometimes that feeling you get at the end of the month when the payment comes due.

The greener grass on the other side usually turns out to be artificial turf. —C.W.H.

Nostalgia is like a grammar lesson: you find the present tense, and the past perfect.

Secretary, taking dictation, to boss: "Are you sure you want an exclamation point? Nobody's surprised at anything anymore."

ONLY A MEDIOCRE PERSON IS ALWAYS AT HIS BEST.

Horsepower was much safer when only horses had it.

If you think you're confused, consider poor Columbus. He didn't know where he was going; when he got there, he didn't know where he was; and when he got back, he didn't know where he'd been.

It takes just as much energy and will to say no to Christ as it does to say yes. —D. L. Moody.

The best night spot in the world is a comfortable bed.

When a painter was once asked, "What is your best painting?" he calmly replied, "My next one."

Tact is the ability to make your guests feel at home when you wish they were.

Overwhelmed is an unusual word. I never heard of anyone being "underwhelmed," or just simply "whelmed." —C.W.H.

You heard of the friendly undertaker who always signed his letters, "Eventually yours."

⎽⎺⎽

One should try to drive so that his license will expire before he does.

⎽⎺⎽

The warden of a Midwest prison sent a note around to inmates asking for suggestions on the kind of party they'd recommend to celebrate his 25th anniversary. The prisoners all had the same idea—OPEN HOUSE.

⎽⎺⎽

A bad cold is both positive and negative. Sometimes the "eyes" have it, and sometimes the "nose."

⎽⎺⎽

Dieting is for people who are thick and tired of it.

⎽⎺⎽

God must have loved a little humor, seeing He made the monkey and the parrot and some of you folks. —Billy Sunday.

⎽⎺⎽

Someone said, "God gave us memory that we might have roses in December."

⎽⎺⎽

Chewing gum proves that you can have motion without progress.

⎽⎺⎽

HORSE SENSE IS STABLE THINKING.

⎽⎺⎽

Sign on a restaurant: "Don't Stand Outside Disgusted; Come In and Get Fed Up."

⌐mm⌐

"Hallelujah" is the one word that is common to all languages. It is never translated. No doubt it is a word that strayed away from Heaven, and we will doubtless continue its use up there. Hallelujah!

⌐mm⌐

If you are a Christian, God needs you! If you are not a Christian, you need God!

⌐mm⌐

Always carry your own light and you will never be in the dark.

⌐mm⌐

Maybe the reason the dog is known as man's best friend is that he gives no advice, never tries to borrow money and has no in-laws.

⌐mm⌐

PLAN AHEAD—NOAH DIDN'T BUILD THE ARK IN THE RAIN.

⌐mm⌐

You cannot sell anything you do not believe in.

⌐mm⌐

No man has a good enough memory to be a successful liar. —Lincoln.

⌐mm⌐

Any person who accepts favors from others is placing a mortgage on his peace of mind.

⌐mm⌐

No matter what a man's past may have been, his future is spotless. —John R. Rice.

⸺

If you could make all men think alike, it would be very much as if no man thought at all. —Phillips Brooks.

⸺

"Lord, we can't hold much, but we can overflow lots!" (From a black minister's prayer.)

⸺

THE BEST GLUE CAN'T MEND A BROKEN PROMISE.

⸺

The last complete, accurate weather forecast was probably when God told Noah that there was a 100% chance of rain.

⸺

Loneliness has its roots, not in the isolation of space, but in the alienation of people.

⸺

It takes as much energy to wish as to plan.

⸺

Dr. B. R. Lakin used to say, "I have a clean mind; I change it often."

⸺

And then there was the fellow who ate in a cafeteria where they make coffee the old-fashioned way—they urn it!

⸺

The car may have replaced the horse, but we have yet to see any bronze statues of generals behind a steering wheel.

I can go a long ways with a man who is wrong in judgment and right in spirit, but it is difficult to travel with one who is right in judgment but wrong in spirit.

Be a patient pedestrian and avoid being a pedestrian patient.

You cannot fool all the people all the time, but those highway interchange signs come pretty close!

One thing about today's individualists is that they are getting harder and harder to tell apart.

I'm neither for nor against apathy.

For a complete list of books available from the Sword of the Lord, write to Sword of the Lord Publishers, P. O. Box 1099, Murfreesboro, Tennessee 37133.